Acclaim for Judy Reiser's Books

"Everyone has his or her own quirk—a crazy bit of behavior that he'd just as soon have no one know about. To give her fellow Americans the feeling that they're not alone, as well as a chance to chortle or smirk at others' idiosyncrasies, Judy Reiser has collected some gem-like examples."

—*The New York Times Book Review*

"Quirks cut across the boundaries of sex, income, race and marital status. Everybody has them. Reiser got grown people to think about it, and to tell her about it."

—*The Washington Post*

"Within minutes I found myself laughing out loud at the confessions that are revealed. Its content will be well received by anyone from the ages of 6–106."

—myshelf.com

"Great stress reliever. Gotta have just for the laughs. Would LOVE to have been on that book's research team!"

—Karla Skinner, amazon.com reviewer

"If you're one of the crazy people, you have the sympathy of myself and all us other normal ones. I'm finished with the column now, so I can go home, as soon as I tap the space bar seven times."

—Bob Greene

"It is not often you come across a book that makes you laugh out loud on practically every page. Judy Reiser's little book does. It is nice to know that you are not alone in some of your own crazy behaviors, and to chortle or smirk at those of others."

—Reese Danley-Kilgo, *The Huntsv*

"This is the funniest book I've read in a long time. You are definitely going to find yourself at least once, possibly numerous times, in here."

—Lisa D'Angelo, bookreviewcafe.com

"A delightfully amusing book. You will have many ah ha! moments, thinking to yourself, 'I do that!'"

—heartlandreviews.com

"These habits provide an amusing reminder of both the variety of human experience and the comfort obtained from such rituals. They give adults a sense of control, and perhaps the same feeling of security a favorite blanket or cuddly toy provides to a toddler."

—Lynne Lamberg, *Books for Sleepless Nights*

Also by Judy Reiser

And I Thought I Was Crazy!

QUIRKS, IDIOSYNCRASIES, AND IRRATIONAL BEHAVIOR

JUDY REISER

PEOPLE DO THE DARNDEST THINGS!

**Andrews McMeel
Publishing**

Kansas City

05 06 07 08 09 FFG 10 9 8 7 6 5 4 3 2 1

ISBN: 0-7407-5109-3

Library of Congress Control Number: 2004111534

Poems, except the last one, by May Rose Salkin

Book design by Holly Camerlinck

Attention: Schools and Businesses
Andrews McMeel books are available at quantity discounts with
bulk purchase for educational, business, or sales promotional use.
For information, please write to: Special Sales Department,
Andrews McMeel Publishing, 4520 Main Street,
Kansas City, Missouri 64111.

To my contributors.
Thank you.

Our house is being painted.
Every time I pass a door,
I get an urge to touch it
When I never did before.

—May Rose Salkin

Contents

Introduction

Do you refuse to take the top newspaper on a stack (even if it's perfect)? Insist that the toilet paper hang "over"? Wait for the phone to ring at least twice before answering even if you're next to it? Pick up a piece of candy you dropped, carefully examine it, blow on it to remove any trace of germs, and then eat it?

You're not alone.

I should know. I interviewed over two thousand people about their quirks and idiosyncrasies for *Admit It, You're Crazy!* and for my first book, *And I Thought I Was Crazy!* These are a few common quirks in which otherwise normal individuals indulge. People do the darndest things!

Revealed within these pages you will find classic and unconventional quirks about food, money, bathrooms, clothing, sleep, germs, and more. Some of our quirks are very funny, some of them are strange, some are charming, and some are damn good ideas! All of them are very human, intriguing, tasteful, and absolutely true. Quirks transcend gender, age, race, nationality, income, and marital status. Everybody's got 'em!

Some idiosyncrasies you might be slightly embarrassed about, others you claim sole ownership of because of their ingeniousness. People will either think of you fondly because of them, or it will irk the hell out of them, and they won't want to have anything to do with you. Let's face it, they're what make you, you.

Here's one a lot of you guys may recognize: When you get dressed, you put on your pants, zip up the zipper, button the button, and buckle the belt. *Then* you get your shirt, unbuckle the belt, unbutton the button, unzip the zipper, tuck your shirt in, and do the whole thing up again. Why don't you put your shirt on first!!!?

Ladies, don't laugh. We may dress more efficiently, but we're just as quirky as the guys: In a social situation, women usually go to the ladies' room in pairs or groups. If two couples are out to dinner and one of the women excuses herself to go to the ladies' room, the chances are pretty good the other woman will go with her. Can you imagine a guy doing this? "Hey, Charlie, I'm going to the men's room. Wanna come with me?"

This book is not attempting to solve, define, or make excuses for some of the more common or uncommon idiosyncrasies. Its intent is simply to help you recognize them, laugh at them, and breathe a little easier. It should comfort you that you're not the only one who:

- orders a big, greasy hamburger and fries, then washes it down with a Diet Coke.

- goes to the gym to exercise but requests a top locker so you won't have to bend down.

- spends hundreds of dollars without giving it a second thought but will not buy Tropicana orange juice unless it's on special.

- flips through a magazine at a newsstand, then reaches for a fresh copy to buy because the one you were flipping through is no longer new.

Admit it, you're crazy!

Loo-ney Tales

You squeeze at the bottom,
I squeeze at the top,
May this fight for supremacy,
Not ever stop.

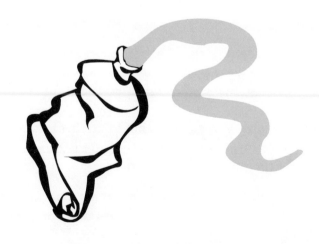

MEN NEED TO FIND SOMETHING to read before entering the bathroom, no matter how badly they have to go. My husband will literally run around with his pants halfway down, trying to find reading material. Women, on the other hand, are in and out in two minutes at the most. Only on rare occasions do we bring reading material in with us. And if we do bring something in to read, like a letter that may have just arrived in the mail, most times we'll be out of the bathroom before we've finished reading the letter!

BOOKKEEPER, FEMALE, 45

HER HUSBAND: JEWELER/JEWELRY BUSINESS OWNER, 47

I CAN'T SIT DOWN on the toilet without something to read. I usually keep a bunch of magazines and books in the bathroom. If there is no reading material in the bathroom, I will actually risk an accident running around the house for something to read. I'll read anything—it could be something I've already read or even cleaning labels if I'm desperate.

ELECTRICAL ENGINEER, MALE, 29

A FRIEND OF MINE marked all the faucets in his house with a little piece of colored tape so that he could turn them to the exact desired temperature with just one twist. When he takes a shower all he has to do is turn the hot knob three quarters of a turn and the cold one a quarter of a turn to the tape and it's exactly the right temperature.

EDITORIAL ASSISTANT FOR A PUBLISHER, MALE, 23

HIS FRIEND: STOCKBROKER, 26

ONE DAY I needed to get my makeup out of the bathroom while my husband was in there taking a shower. I reached in to get my makeup bag, being careful not to let the steam out or the cold air in. Out of the corner of my eye I glanced toward the shower—we have clear sliding glass doors—and noticed my husband using his two hands to squeegee his body semidry. He was working his way down his body from his head. The water was turned off at this point. I asked him, "What are you doing?" And he said, "Oh, nuthin." I said, "Are you squeegeeing your body with your hands to get all the water off?" He goes, "So?" I was amazed.

RADIO TALK SHOW HOST, FEMALE, 34

HER HUSBAND: AIR TRAFFIC CONTROLLER, 34

MY DAD would always put a safety pin at the end of his bath towel so he would know which end to use for his face and which end to use for his feet! I used to tease him about it whenever I visited. I would check all the towels for safety pins!

GRAPHIC DESIGNER, FEMALE, 50

HER DAD: PRODUCTION COORDINATOR FOR A WOMEN'S CLOTHING MANUFACTURER, DECEASED

My wife and I use two different toothpaste tubes because I like mine squeezed from the bottom to the top perfectly and my wife squishes from the middle.

STRUCTURAL ENGINEER, MALE, 35

EACH TIME I TEAR OFF a piece of toilet paper, I fold it in the opposite direction from the way it is curled onto the roll. When you roll it in the opposite direction, you are rolling it against the grain, so to speak, which causes the tissue to spread out more, making it slightly more coarse, and according to my personal experience, more grabby and absorbent. You can see the difference with a magnifying glass. I also pull off exactly five squares at a time, every time.

PHOTOGRAPHER, MALE, 49

WHEN WE PLAY CARDS, if we're on a winning streak, we continue to play and we won't get up for anything, not even to go to the bathroom, no matter how badly we have to go. If we hit a losing streak, we all get up and go to the bathroom even if we don't have to go. We'll wash our hands or something just to get away from the bad streak.

ACCOUNTANT, MALE, 32

I DON'T LIKE USING COMBS, I only use brushes. I don't really feel comfortable with combs—they're just not as friendly. They're sort of disturbing.

STUDENT, SENIOR, MALE, 20

MY WIFE has a weird habit every night of putting toothpaste on her toothbrush even though she's not planning to brush her teeth for a while. She goes out of the bathroom and leaves the toothbrush with the toothpaste on it sitting on the counter for three or four hours.

ACCOUNT SUPERVISOR, PUBLIC RELATIONS, MALE, 31
HIS WIFE: MARKETING DIRECTOR, FURNITURE COMPANY, 28

MY UNUSUAL RITUAL is that I put on all my makeup before I take a shower. My makeup regimen includes mascara, eye-liner, eye shadow, face base, lipstick, and frequently, lip liner. I completely finish putting on my makeup and only then do I step into the shower (where I also wash my hair). The makeup doesn't run since I don't take piping hot showers. For the hair-washing segment, I turn my back to the showerhead and wash my hair with my head tilted back, as you would in a beauty shop with your head propped back on the sink.

I'm not exactly sure why this ritual started, but I do know that I've been doing this for almost thirty years. As a humorous side note, many years ago I was watching one of those fictional detective shows on television and, in one episode, a woman was found dead in her shower. All the investigators were in her apartment sizing up the situation. One of the detectives said, "Well, we know she must have been killed somewhere else and then dragged into the shower because she has all her makeup on." They all nodded in agreement at this clever, deductive reasoning and I thought, "Boy, little do they know."

ADMINISTRATIVE ASSISTANT, FEMALE, 52

I RECENTLY told a friend about my interesting little makeup/shower habit, which I contributed to your book. She thought it was so weird that I apply my makeup before shower-ing. I asked her if there was anything she did that was equally odd. She said absolutely not, except . . . possibly, for the fact that when she goes to the bathroom she always counts (one, two, three . . .) and tries to end her peeing on an even number. I have absolutely no idea why she enumerates while she urinates.

HER FRIEND: No real purpose behind any of it. I don't know why I do it—I just do it. I find that I count when I do a lot of things. I guess I'm just trying to keep busy.

ADMINISTRATIVE ASSISTANT, FEMALE, 52

HER FRIEND: SPECIAL EDUCATION TEACHER, 52

I FLUSH THE TOILET before I'm done relieving myself because I'm having this race. I remember specifically why I do it. The race was established when I was a child. My father and I were in a competition to see who could go quicker. He got tired of that race, so he told me to race against the flush instead. Although I'm now fifty, I still do it.

SALES REPRESENTATIVE FOR PRINTER, MALE, 50

I HAVE TO SPREAD THE TOOTHPASTE across the full width of the bristles of the toothbrush. If it doesn't extend across the full width, I'll wash it off and start again or I won't brush my teeth.

OFFICE ASSISTANT, MALE, 24

OUR HOUSE HAS THREE BATHROOMS. All the toilet seats are identical yet I'm only comfortable in one of the bathrooms. Sometimes, even though it's urgent, I'll wait if that bathroom is occupied. I feel like Goldilocks and the Three Bears . . . the one in the hallway is too big; the one downstairs is too small; but the third one is juuuussst right.

RESTAURATEUR, MALE, 58

WHEN I GO TO THE DRUGSTORE to buy a new toothbrush, I stand in front of the rack, stare at all the colors, and have a major conversation with myself. Which is a happy color? Which color haven't I had for a while? What color am I in the mood for today? I don't match the toothbrush to the color of the bathroom. I try not to repeat toothbrush colors frequently. I take this very seriously. I do the same with cards and wrapping paper—it has to be just right.

OWNER, GARMENT BUSINESS, FEMALE, 40S

MY HUSBAND IS A TOILET PAPER ROLLER. He must be able to grab the toilet paper and roll it around his hand and rip it off very easily. Standard toilet paper holders that are sold on the market just don't do the job for him. So he designed and built his own toilet paper holder himself out of plumbing supplies. It looks like an L-shaped hook, which protrudes from the wall. The toilet paper sits on top of the hook part.

JR: Have you become a roller too?

No, I've always been a crumpler and have remained a crumpler.

NURSE, FEMALE, 31

HER HUSBAND: COMPUTER PROGRAMMER, 30

I HAVE TO USE A CLEAN TOWEL every day after showering. When I think about it, what a waste that is because I've just dried a clean body. A bath towel could be used two or three times at least. But no way can I use a bath towel on Tuesday that I've dried myself with on Monday.

SYNDICATED RADIO BROADCASTER, MALE, 43

I CANNOT USE A STALL AT WORK if I see a guy walk out of it before me. I have to imagine to myself that I am the only one who will use that toilet for the day.

JR: What if you really have to go?

I hold it. I will leave the bathroom and wait awhile, then go back and hope that I do not see anyone walk out of the stall again. I am not kidding.

CONSULTANT, BUSINESS PLANS FOR SMALL START-UP BUSINESSES, MALE, 29

I ALWAYS TAKE THREE PAPER TOWELS in a public rest room. If there is a paper towel machine that has a lever, I always pump the lever in multiples of three. I have no idea where the three paper towels came from. It's not lost on me that three and four are both factors of twelve, which is my favorite number, but I don't think that has anything to do with its origin. I think it's just something I noticed that I did naturally and started making a conscious choice.

MBA STUDENT, MALE, 26

Whenever I get a haircut, I go home, wet my hair, and completely recomb it because I never like the way it looks when the barber styles it. It doesn't matter who the barber is or how skilled he is—I recomb it.

POLICE OFFICER, MALE, 37

I HAVEN'T USED TOILET PAPER IN TWO YEARS.

JR: What do you use?

I use baby wipes. If I have to go to the bathroom after I get out of the shower, I feel like going right back into the shower. With baby wipes, I feel like I just came out of the shower. My wife told me about it when we were dating. She uses them and I tried it after she recommended them. I've been using them ever since. I carry them with me. You can't throw a baby wipe in the toilet—it's not biodegradable, so I use toilet paper first and then finish with the baby wipes.

ELECTRICIAN, MALE, 31

MY EX-HUSBAND AND I had a discussion years ago about how one uses the toilet paper. He divided people into two groups, the crumplers and the folders. He was obviously a folder but I didn't know how much of a folder until years later when one of my children revealed that my ex-husband marched five of our six children, ranging in age from about eight to sixteen at the time, into a very small bathroom. He then demonstrated, dead seriously, the proper way—the only way—to utilize toilet paper. He explained to them that a sheet of four squares of toilet paper should be ripped off, folded into one square and then folded twice again. This, he instructed, is the only way to do it and there are no other options.

JR: Have your kids adopted this method?
They absolutely refuse to discuss it with me. I've asked them that question. They say, "It's not your business, Mom."

JR: How about you? Are you a folder or a crumpler?
For the record, I'm a crumpler.

ORTHOPEDIC SURGEON, FEMALE, 53

HER EX-HUSBAND: CARDIAC SURGEON, 57

I HAVE TWO HOOKS IN THE BATHROOM that I use for underwear rotation. I go into the bathroom and take off the underwear that I've been wearing that day and hang it on the right hook. The next day when I take off the underwear that I've been wearing that day, I hang it on the left hook. After I shower I take the underwear that's hanging on the right hook and put it in the laundry bag. The rotation continues.

JR: Where is the fresh underwear?
In my drawer.

STUDENT, MALE, 23

I MUST TAKE A BUBBLE BATH every single night. That's how I relax. If we're on vacation, we don't check into a hotel that only has a stall shower.

SENIOR VICE PRESIDENT, BANKING, FEMALE, "BETWEEN 35 AND 50"

I SHAVE IN FRONT OF THE TV because that way I can watch TV while being productive at the same time.

ACCOUNTANT, MALE, 24

IT DOESN'T MATTER that I've just gotten out of the shower and I am completely clean from head to toe, if I do something with my hands and then wash them, I have to rinse my face as well. I don't know why.

RADIO CALLER, MALE, PROFESSION AND AGE UNKNOWN

WHEN I GO TO THE BATHROOM at home and no one other than my family is present, I leave the door open. With the door open, I don't feel the need to turn on the light. I prefer to go in the dark.

REPORTER, MALE, 42

I MUST USE MOUTHWASH before I brush, never after. Mouthwash discolors the teeth. The idea of brushing is to get everything off the teeth.

FOREIGN GOVERNMENT EMPLOYEE, MALE, 41

I STARTED TO BRUSH MY TEETH with my left hand about two years ago even though I'm right-handed, just to see if I could do it. And now, two years later, I still brush with my left hand.

JR: Are you doing as good a job?
Yes, if not better.

JR: Did you try doing anything else with your left hand?
I tried eating with it but it took too long and I didn't get to eat enough.

JR: So you're not ambidextrous yet?
Not at all.

FINANCIAL PLANNER, MALE, 22

EVERY DAY I BRING MY PANTIES, bra, and stockings into the shower with me and wash them with soap and water as I'm showering. In addition to being a real time-saver, my under-garments last longer by hand-washing them.

INTERNET STRATEGIST, FEMALE, 32

I ALWAYS END MY SHOWER with about three minutes of cold water because I drink the water directly from the showerhead to hydrate myself for the day. I probably drink a couple of glasses' worth. I also do it because according to family legend, my great-grandfather deliberately never used hot water to remind himself how poor he was at one time.

MARKETING/CREATIVE SERVICES RESEARCH SPECIALIST, MALE, 36

I'LL ONLY USE A TOILET in a public bathroom if the stalls on either side of the one I'm using are empty. I cannot go if some-one is directly next to me. If there are three stalls, and there's a guy on the left and a guy on the right and the middle one is unoccupied, even if I have to go very badly, I'll wait. I feel that I would be invading their space and they would be invading my space. You cannot pee in comfort unless every other stall is empty. You're marking your territory—you can't have somebody just sit right next to you like that.

TECHNICIAN, COMMUNICATIONS, MALE, 34

ALL THE TOOTHBRUSHES on my stand have to be facing in the same direction, to the left. Left is luckier for me.

HOUSEWIFE, FEMALE, 40

I BUY TOILET PAPER IN DIFFERENT COLORS because I like variety. I don't match the color to my bathroom décor. When I finish a roll, I select the color that I'm in the mood for at that moment. There's a store near me that sells blue, beige, and pink toilet paper. It only comes in single ply but it's a bigger roll.

ACTRESS, 43

WHEN I SHOWER I wash my entire body first and then I shampoo my hair last. I like to wash my entire body first and then attack the biggest, dirtiest part at the end.

LAWYER, MALE, 29

I LOOK INSIDE PEOPLE'S MEDICINE CABINETS when I use their bathroom because I'm curious to see what medications they take and what else they have. It's fascinating sometimes.

WRITER/JOURNALIST, MALE, 31

I USE A FRESH TOWEL EACH DAY to dry myself off with after showering. The previous day's towel is used to wipe down the shower stall. I put the one that I've dried myself with on the rack inside the shower and the clean towel on the outside rack so that I can differentiate between them but sometimes I still get confused.

JR: You must have a lot of laundry.
Well, my wife worries about that.

JR: Does your wife use the same system?
I don't think so.

ELECTRICAL FIELD ENGINEER, MALE, 39

MY HUSBAND has to bring a pair of clean underwear into the bathroom when he's about to take a shower. He won't even turn on the water until the underwear is in place. My ten-year-old son now does the same thing. Occasionally, when I've just done laundry and the clothes are still in the dryer, I'll tell one or the other to go ahead and shower—I'll bring in the underwear when they're dry. No deal, that water stays off until I appear with the underwear.

BOOKKEEPER, FEMALE, 45
HER HUSBAND: JEWELER/JEWELRY BUSINESS OWNER, 47
HER SON: FIFTH-GRADE STUDENT, 10

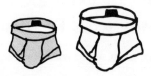

BEFORE I GO TO BED, I brush, I floss, and then I brush again.

HOTEL DEVELOPER, MALE, 32

I HAVE TO SHOWER before getting into bed. If I've showered at 3:00 A.M. before leaving the house and get back at 5:00 A.M., I can't sleep without a shower. And I absolutely will not lie on the bed without a shower. I will lie on the floor instead.

ADMINISTRATIVE ASSISTANT, FEMALE, 33

I HAVE SEVEN SETS OF TOWELS, each in a different color. I pick a different color set every day according to my mood.

TEXTILE DESIGNER, FEMALE, 23

MY DENTIST TELLS ME that you're supposed to brush your teeth for two minutes. Two minutes is longer than you think it is. So I walk all around the house, watch some TV, go back, spit in the sink and then walk around the house some more. I do that for about two minutes, brushing the entire time. We have an hourglass that the dentist gave my wife, which is a two-minute timer. My teeth aren't very white but I don't have cavities.

EXECUTIVE RECRUITER, MALE, 31

Every time my friend takes a shower, he brings a five-gallon bucket into the shower with him. During his shower the bucket fills up with excess water, which he then uses to flush his toilet.

RADIO CALLER, MALE, PROFESSION AND AGE UNKNOWN

WHEN MY KIDS WERE LITTLE they required a lot of attention as most little kids do, so time became a very valuable commodity.

As a result I could never spare the time for a leisurely shower and it was extremely hard to find the time to shave my legs. So I shaved one leg one day and the other leg another day. Sometimes by the time I got to the second leg, the first leg was already hairy and needed to be shaved again. No two legs were ever clean-shaven at the same time. That went on for many years and frequently still does because I still don't have enough time.

HEALTH WRITER, FEMALE, 46

SOMETIMES I PEE in the shower. I don't really think it's a big deal.

CREATIVE DIRECTOR, FEMALE, 40

I BRING MY TOOTHBRUSH and toothpaste into the shower with me and brush my teeth in the shower. Even if I've brushed my teeth earlier, when I get into the shower later on, I'll brush my teeth again.

SCRIPT SUPERVISOR, FILM INDUSTRY, FEMALE, 47

IF I USE A PARTICULAR BRAND OF SHAMPOO I must use the exact same brand of hair spray, conditioner, gel, or any other hairdressing. For example, if I use Suave shampoo, then I must use Suave hair spray. I can't bring myself to use a different brand although there are several different brands in the house and I know they're all probably the same or very similar. It just doesn't seem right to use a brand that doesn't match.

RESTAURATEUR, MALE, 58

I WILL NOT SING IN THE SHOWER before I eat breakfast because if you sing before breakfast, you cry before dinner. To get around this dilemma, sometimes before I go into the shower, I'll go in the kitchen and eat a couple of crackers or a piece of fruit and then I can sing to my heart's content while I wash myself.

RELATIONSHIP MANAGER, ADVERTISING SOFTWARE, MALE, 41

EVERY TIME I GO TO A RESTAURANT or walk into any building where I'm going to be for a while, I have to go to the bathroom first. It's a habit. A Pavlovian thing. Conditioning. I want to be relaxed for whatever I'm going to do.

JOURNALIST, MALE, 39

ONE OF LIFE'S GREATEST simple pleasures is to have a cold beer in a hot shower.

JOURNALIST, FINANCIAL MAGAZINE, MALE, 30

WHEN I BATHE, I always use one side of the washcloth for my body and the other side for my face. No exceptions. I keep it flat on one hand and put the soap right on the cloth and I don't let it get crunched up so I won't get confused. After I've washed my face, I flip the washcloth over, move the soap, and wash my body.

LAWYER, MALE, 28

I BLOW-DRY MY FEET EVERY MORNING. Towel drying still leaves my feet a little damp and I hate putting damp feet into my shoes. Blow-drying dries them thoroughly and they're ready to enter shoes.

MARKETING ACCOUNT EXECUTIVE, FEMALE, 25

I USE ABOUT A DOZEN TOOTHBRUSHES. I choose one each night depending on my mood. I have the soft; the hard; the small; the big; the foreign ones; the domestic ones; different-colored ones, and I rotate among them. I use some frequently—two or three times every week—and others are used infrequently, every month or so. The soft ones are my favorite. The color doesn't matter as much; it's just for aesthetics. The quality of the toothbrush is what matters.

COMPUTER TECHNICIAN, MALE, 32

WE DIDN'T HAVE A SHOWER when I was growing up, so I'm accustomed to taking baths. Now that I do have a shower, I always take a bath first and then a shower. I never quite got used to taking a shower, so I find myself sitting in the tub, taking a bath and then getting up and showering off all the dirty water I've been sitting in. Occasionally, when I'm away from home and the bathroom doesn't have a tub, I'm tempted to sit down in the stall shower—but I can't quite bring myself to do it.

MANAGER, HOSPITAL EKG AND PHLEBOTOMY DEPARTMENT, FEMALE, 46

WHEN I SIT ON THE TOILET at home, I have to take off my top, whether it's a T-shirt or button-down shirt, because I'm paranoid that the end of the shirt is going to fall into the toilet bowl. It's easier to take it off than hold it up.

PROFESSION UNKNOWN, MALE, 27

IF I'M IN MY APARTMENT by myself and I see something scary on TV or if I'm reading a book and I get spooked, I have to make sure nothing is behind the shower curtain. I open the shower curtain and leave it open.

COMPUTER GRAPHIC ARTIST, FEMALE, 27

I SCRAPE ALL THE TOOTHPASTE from the end right up to where the nozzle is with the end of my toothbrush. The tube has to be nice and flat and smooth. Once I've done that for a few days, I give up on that and take a pair of scissors from the kitchen and cut the end of the tube off. Then I swirl my brush around inside the tube. It's amazing—you can get three or four more days' worth of toothpaste out of it.

STOCKBROKER, MALE, 24

I'M A GUY who has to use my own facilities at home. Before I leave the house, I use my own bathroom. I may have acquired this quirk from my experience in the army.

JR: What do you do when you're traveling?
When I'm in a motel or away from home, I have a difficult time. I take my own spray.

RADIO CALLER, MALE, PROFESSION AND AGE UNKNOWN

MY WIFE AND I have a recurring argument about which is the correct side to open the sliding glass doors to get into the shower. I argue that the correct side is where the faucet is because you can test the water temperature and then get right in. And when you get out, the towel is there and that's where the mat should go. My wife argues that you should get in on the other side, which is farther from the water, so the floor doesn't get wet.

JR: Who wins?
It's ongoing and undecided.

SOFTWARE ENGINEER, IT FIRM, MALE, 30

I PURPOSELY LEAVE THE TOILET PAPER on the back of the toilet. I don't hang it on the holder. It's easier. It probably started out of laziness and I got used to it. My roommates are also too lazy to bother hanging it up. If someone does hang it up, I'll just grab another roll from under the sink.

COMPUTER CONSULTANT, MALE, 31

I SHAVE IN THE OFFICE instead of in my house. I don't have time to shave at home because I'm usually rushing to catch the train. I get my coffee and newspaper as I get on the train. I keep my shaving kit in a bathroom at the office that nobody knows about. It's an abandoned bathroom in really horrible condition. Every day I get in at about 8:30 A.M. and go in there and shave for about ten minutes on company time. Otherwise I'd have to get up ten minutes earlier. They'd probably be upset if they knew I was doing it.

CIVIL ENGINEER, MALE, 33

After I'm finished using a public urinal or public bathroom, I have to spit into the toilet. I have no idea why I do it. I've been doing it for as long as I can remember— each and every time—sometimes twice.

SOUND DESIGNER, MALE, 33

AT WORK OR IN A PUBLIC BATHROOM that I use frequently, if someone is in the stall that I typically use, I will turn around and leave and then come back later. There are three stalls at work and I always use the middle one.

ENVIRONMENTAL ENGINEER, MALE, 32

ONE DAY A WEEK, I take a shower for an hour and a half but on all other days I take a five-minute shower. I never know which day of the week I will take the longer shower—it's whenever the mood strikes me.

STUDENT, MALE, 23

I HAVE NOTICED that this behavior is common among men: When using the stall (not the urinal) in a public men's room, upon hearing someone else enter the room, most men let out an audible cough or some other noise. (I prefer to blow my nose.) I call it the *Territorial Toilet Cough*.

I asked my wife if women do the same thing. Her reply was to look at me like I was crazy (which I'll assume is a no).

I'm not a psychologist, but I think the reasoning behind it is that men prefer to do their bathroom thing as far away from other men as possible (e.g., the unwritten rule of *never* using a urinal next to one that is occupied unless it is the only one available). Making someone aware of your presence will ensure that they will use the appropriate (farthest) stall.

DIRECTOR OF INFORMATION SYSTEMS, MALE, 33

HIS WIFE: HOMEMAKER, 34

MY FRIEND DOESN'T DRY HER HANDS with a paper towel when she washes her hands because she doesn't like the way the paper smells. She just lets her hands air dry.

FASHION DESIGNER, FEMALE, 23

HER FRIEND: IN FABRIC MERCHANDISING, FEMALE, 22

AFTER A SHOWER, a very good friend of mine doesn't wipe himself off with the towel the way most people normally do. He wraps the towel around his body as if he's getting warm in a blanket and allows the water to be absorbed into the towel. He'll do that all over his body in three or four wrappings until he's done.

ACADEMIC ADMINISTRATOR, MALE, 29

HIS FRIEND: SCIENTIST, BIOTECH INDUSTRY, 29

I READ MY MAIL while sitting in the bathroom. I open it, read it, and discard what I don't need. It just kills time while I'm sitting there doing my business. I don't have time to read magazines, so I don't subscribe to them.

COMPUTER TECHNICIAN, MALE, 29

ANYTIME I'M IN THE SHOWER and I soap up my underarms, I have to wash them off six or seven times because it freaks me out to step out of the shower and still have soap under my underarms. It throws my whole day off.

FINANCIAL REPRESENTATIVE, MALE, 21

BEFORE I GET IN THE SHOWER in the morning I have to prepare everything that I will need to use when I get out of the shower. I take the razor and shaving cream out and put toothpaste on the toothbrush. When I get out of the shower I have a sequence of events that is ready to go.

ATTORNEY, MALE, 36

I LIKE TO BRUSH MY TEETH before I eat so that I can enjoy the flavor of the food, and I also brush my teeth after I eat so that it doesn't feel like there's a basset hound in my mouth. If I eat out I just have to hang on until I get home and the first thing I do after stepping inside is brush my teeth.

REGISTERED NURSE, FEMALE, 33

PRIOR TO LEAVING ON A TRIP out of town my bathrooms must be cleaned from top to bottom. Mirrors are Windexed, tubs are scrubbed, garbage cans are emptied, floors are cleaned, sinks are wiped down (no water droplets!), rugs are straightened, fresh towels are put on all towel bars, and the liquid-soap bottles are refilled. It annoys me to come home to a dirty, unorganized bathroom!

RETAIL, FEMALE, 30

At this stage of my life, as I'm approaching forty, I've become lazy, so now I sit down to pee. I've been doing this for the last three to four years. At work I use the urinal because I don't feel that the toilet is as hygienically clean. But after work, I'm too tired to stand.

BOND SALESMAN, MALE, 38

Funny Money

Messy, wrinkled money
Is no appealing sight.
But if it is a fifty,
Clean or wrinkled, it's all right.

I HAVE NO PROBLEM spending upward of $300 on shoes or pants—any type of designer clothing—but when it comes to simple necessities, if I go to the drugstore and buy a hair gel for $3.10—like, hey, that's outrageous!

LEGAL ASSISTANT, MALE, 23

Many people arrange their money in order of denomination. So do I. But I also arrange it in order, by letter, A through whatever.

HIGH-SCHOOL STUDENT, FEMALE, 16

MY VEHICLES have to be completely organized before I can drive with a clear conscience. Kind of like flight attendants who insist that, "Everything must be completely underneath the seat in front of you before takeoff." I have one of those combination change, drink, cassette, and miscellaneous slot caddies that goes on the floor of the car over the hump.

The change holders (which are all sized perfectly for quarters, dimes, and nickels, but with no place for pennies—that really bugs me) must be fully stocked with change, the heads on all the coins must be faceup and the faces must be as close to going all the same way as possible. After long highway trips vibration usually shifts the faces. They must be realigned when I get home. This change is not to be used. I will dig through my wallet for the correct amount of change or just get change back before I'll use that money. My husband has made the mistake of using that change for tolls when I wasn't quick enough. He paid the price, let me tell you. Need I say more . . . ?

RADIO TALK SHOW HOST, FEMALE, 34

HER HUSBAND: AIR TRAFFIC CONTROLLER, 34

WHEN I WRITE CHECKS, I frequently pay an additional amount so I'm left with a balance that is an even number in my checkbook. For example, if I get a bill for $25.25 and I have a balance of $135.75, I'll write the check for an amount that leaves me with $110 or $100 when I deduct it from my current balance.

WEB DEVELOPER, MALE, 32

I ALWAYS PICK UP PENNIES—it doesn't matter whether they're heads or tails. There have been times when I've nearly killed myself when I spot a penny and there's onrushing traffic, but I pick it up anyway because I feel that I'm going to be very lucky. My crowning achievement in penny picking was when I went to Sedona, Arizona, where all of the rocks are copper-colored and there nestled in a surface was a penny, heads up, the same color as the rock, with the sun shining on it. I considered that a very fortuitous moment in my life.

TEXTILE DESIGNER, FEMALE, 57

THEY MAY BE FILTHY LITTLE THINGS that aren't worth anything, but it's very unlucky not to pick up pennies on the ground. I'm not at all superstitious about other things. I've trained myself not to pick them up occasionally, but it always nags at me. I know I'm tempting fate if I ever notice a penny and I don't pick it up.

ENGLISH PROFESSOR, COMMUNITY COLLEGE, FEMALE, 49

I HAVE AN AVERSION TO PENNIES—always have. I throw them away because they're useless.

STOCK BOY, MALE, 20

I WON'T BUY ANYTHING FROM ANYONE I don't like. If they do anything to upset me in the process of the buying/selling exchange—it doesn't make a difference what kind of sale it is—I simply will not buy it because it's got bad vibes and will bring bad luck.

ATTORNEY, FEMALE, 32

WHEN I'M FILLING OUT the tip on a restaurant credit card receipt, I'll make the amount of the tip a figure that will result in a round dollar total.

STRATEGIST, INTERNET START-UP COMPANY, MALE, 28

I CHECK THE BALANCE of my checking account approximately ten times during the day just to see whether I can catch a check that's being cashed almost at the moment when it's being done. It gives me satisfaction, for example, to call my bank and hear that check number 211 was cashed when I didn't hear it five minutes ago in my last phone call.

INSURANCE BROKER, MALE, 27

I DON'T LIKE CHANGE. When I buy something I just shove the change in the bottom of my bag and carry it around until my bag gets too heavy and then I take all the change out and put it down in my apartment. My apartment is always full of change, all different currencies, just lying around. Eventually my mum comes to visit me from England and she runs around my apartment collecting it all and putting it into little bags, which she takes with her, spends, or leaves for me. I never spend it.

COMMUNICATIONS OFFICER, FEMALE, 31

EACH TIME I GET A DOLLAR, I have to count the total amount I have saved altogether. When I get money from my tooth fairy, I never spend that money. I'm saving my money until I'm grown up.

STUDENT, FOURTH GRADE, FEMALE, 9

I BELIEVE IN BUYING everything in twos. If I buy a screwdriver and it works the way I like it the first couple of times, then I buy a second one. I keep the second one brand new. I may never use it. If I should ever lose the first one, I'll have another one in the closet. I buy a second pair of shoes in the exact same color and style. If one wears out, I have the other one. I have six computers. I'm in the computer field, so that makes sense. People who know me know that if I buy one thing, I'll buy the same item again later on as a backup.

JR: You must live in a big house?
No, I don't.

JR: If the first one breaks, do you use the second one?
Yes, and then I buy another one just in case that one breaks.

JR: What if that model or style is no longer available?
I get one as close as possible. If nothing similar is available, I'll wear the second one out and buy two more, one to be active and one as a backup.

NETWORK MANAGER, COMPUTERS, MALE, 37

MY FIANCÉ has a weird sense of humor. When he writes a check to be given as a wedding gift, he makes it out for an odd amount as a joke. For example, rather than writing a check for $300.00 or $350.00, he will give the couple $353.02.

ACCOUNTANT, FEMALE, 30

HER FIANCÉ: OPTIONS TRADER, 34

IF I DROP ANY PENNIES on the ground, I turn them heads up before I can pick them up.

MEMBERSHIP, FEMALE, 26

IF I NOTICE A PENNY on the street and it's tails, I will bend down and turn it around so that it's facing heads up but I do not pick it up. I leave it there for the next person who comes along so they will feel lucky.

INTERIOR DESIGNER, FEMALE, 46

I HAVE THIS THEORY going back to seventh grade that lunch—and we're in New York City here—should cost under $5.00. The point of the story is that I will make sure that my lunch costs under $5.00 and that it will still fill me up. Even if I earned $20 million, I would still eat lunch for under $5.00. There's pizza; there's deli sandwiches; there's Middle Eastern food; there's chicken and rice from the carts on the sidewalk for $3.50. I bring the lunch back to the office and drink the water there.

EXECUTIVE RECRUITER, MALE, 31

MY NINETY-THREE-YEAR-OLD grandmother is extremely methodical about her checkbook. Each blank check, based on its number, is reserved for a particular purpose. For example, one time she asked me to purchase a glider-rocker she saw advertised in the paper. After I delivered it to her, she got out her checkbook to reimburse me. She opened the checkbook and flipped through the blank checks one by one, while saying, "This one's for groceries; this one's for the power bill; this one's for rent; this one's for . . ." until she got about halfway through the checkbook and said, "Here's one I can use." Believe it or not, at ninety-three she has all her wits about her. Nobody knows how this quirk of hers started.

BUSINESS ANALYST, MALE, 40

TO RECORD DEPOSITS or checks in my checkbook, I will only write in pencil—no pen whatsoever. It drives my husband crazy. He doesn't understand it. It must be in pencil because it's easier to make a correction and looks neater.

LEGAL SECRETARY, FEMALE, 37

My wife's wrinkled bills are for gasoline.

DOCTOR, MALE, 50

HIS WIFE: HOUSEWIFE, 51

AS A CPA I work with numbers all day long, but I frequently neglect to make sure that I have enough money before going out. I've been known to walk around with just three cents on me and not be aware of it until I reach for my wallet to pay for something. Knowing this, my husband fills my wallet with money every night. He goes through all the money that's in the house and selects the bills that are in the best condition. It's always the same denominations—a twenty, a ten, a five, four singles, three quarters, a dime, two nickels, and five pennies.

So if there's a crummy five and a nice, neat five, he gives me the nice, neat five. I usually spend the money at the grocery store or somewhere else, so the condition of the bills is not important to me, but it is to him.

JR: Has he ever forgotten?
Never.

JR (to husband): Do you put the same combination in your own wallet?
No. There's no set amount that I carry—I'm less idio-syncratic about what I carry than about what my wife carries. Possibly because she needs more order in her life than I do.

JR: What happens if you don't have a particular denomina-tion bill in the house?
It's okay because I'm only 95 percent obsessive compulsive—5 percent of me is relatively well adjusted. We people who are somewhat obsessive compulsive do not always require hospitalization. Sometimes we do things that are productive. This quality enables us to bring order to the world that other people constantly mess up.

CPA, FEMALE, 51

PAROLE OFFICER, MALE, 53

I ALWAYS CARRY SPARE CHANGE so I can round my change to the nearest quarter, because I need quarters for the laundry. Often, when I pay for a purchase and give the cashier additional coins to round up the change, the cashier will ask, "What's this change for?" I always explain, "So I get a quarter back."

WEB SITE PRODUCER, MALE, 28

I PREFER FEMALE blackjack dealers. In fact, I won't sit down at a table where there is a male dealer. And if the shift changes and a male dealer comes on, I'll leave.

JR: Has this system been working for you?

It works pretty well. Even though I know it's not logical, I plan to stick with it. I believe that I lose more money with male dealers.

SYSTEMS ANALYST, MALE, 38

I will only buy a wallet that has two partitions for bills. I put singles and fives in the front and tens, twenties, and everything else in the back.

PARALEGAL, FEMALE, 60

WHEN I WENT TO JAPAN twenty years ago, I noticed that Japanese paper currency was always neatly folded. It was never creased or wrinkled because imperfect bills were quickly taken out of circulation, so most of the bills were brand new. Ever since then, I always make sure that my bills are flat and not folded or wrinkled. It's become a compulsion of some kind.

JR to Reader: He showed them to me. They're very neat.

PAINTER (ARTIST), MALE, 63

A WEALTHY BLUE-BLOODED PATIENT of mine got fed up with giving away a lot of her money on wedding gifts to her many nieces and nephews and then finding out that many of them divorced soon after the wedding. As a result, she no longer gives the full amount of her gift up front. She parcels out the wedding gift in installments according to a pre-determined schedule that takes into consideration the duration of the marriage. She gives the newlyweds the first quarter of the total amount of her gift at the end of the first year of marriage. Five years later, she gives them another quarter if they are still together. And if they are still married after ten years, they get the third quarter. I don't recall how many years after that they finally receive the balance. I'm not sure how much money she gives.

 JR: Does she give anything at the wedding?
Nothing.

GYNECOLOGIST, FEMALE, 54
HER PATIENT: RETIRED, 80s

I'M METICULOUS about balancing my checking statement each month. Even if it's off by just two cents, I must find the mistake no matter how long it takes, which is crazy. There has never been a time that I didn't balance my checking statement.

RETIRED, FEMALE, 89

I ALWAYS RUB lottery tickets off with my lucky coin. It's a dime I found a long time ago that I always keep with me for good luck.

 JR: How many times have you won?
Never.

MOVER, MALE, 41

I PREFER OLD MONEY. Old money has many advantages over new money. It doesn't stick together the way crisp new bills do. I can fold them flatter because they aren't as stiff, so several old bills fit more easily into my change purse than new ones. Old bills have a history and aura because they've traveled around and have come into contact with so many different types of people. And because they've been in circulation for a while, they're not likely to be counterfeit.

RETIRED, FEMALE, 67

APARTMENT DWELLERS will much sooner tell you about their sex lives than reveal how much they tipped the building staff for Christmas. People don't want to be embarrassed to find out that they undertipped or feel like a sucker if they overtipped. Neighbors will try to sniff each other out when they run into each other in the hallway: "How much did you give Louis this year?" But it's useless. They will try to get around it by feigning a memory lapse or saying that their spouse is in charge of the tips or somehow put the ball back in the other person's court. Some people feel good about themselves if they overtip. They think they're going to get the best service.

 JR: Which category do you belong in?

Me . . . I want to know what people are paying because I don't want to pay too much.

PODIATRIST, MALE, 47

I ALWAYS SPEND old bills first. Even my friends have noticed. New is cleaner. You don't know where money's been. I'd rather have it cleaner. The old ones frequently smell like bars.

VICE PRESIDENT, BANKING, MALE, 39

IF I HAVE FIVE DIFFERENT CHECKS, I make five different deposits into my bank account—one for each check—rather than combine them all. When I get the statement, this enables me to see each amount and then I can trace it back to where I got it.

SYSTEMS ENGINEER, MALE, 28

Often, I'll give away five nickels in return for two dimes because I hate change in my pocket.

EXECUTIVE VICE PRESIDENT, COMMERCIAL REAL ESTATE, MALE, 44

I'LL NEVER ACCEPT a bill that has a piece torn off or is ripped or defective in any way. I'm afraid that it won't be accepted when I pay for something.

PROJECT ENGINEER, MALE, 34

BEFORE MY FRIEND'S FATHER plays the slot machine, he always does a little dance in front of the machine and bows in homage to the machine. He does mock pulls of the lever a couple of times before actually pulling it the third time. This is all for good luck.

JR: Is he usually lucky?

Not really.

TEACHER, MALE, 32
HIS FRIEND'S FATHER: SANITATION WORKER, 60

MY FRIEND CALCULATES that she's really earning half as much as she's actually earning because taxes take half of it. If she earns fifty dollars, she'll tell you that she only made twenty-five dollars. However, if she's spending money, she's spending with after-tax dollars, so she believes that she is spending twice the amount. If she buys sheets for twenty-five dollars, she believes that they really cost her fifty dollars.

LAWYER, FEMALE, 52

HER FRIEND: LAWYER, FEMALE, 61

I NEVER BALANCE my checkbook but I always keep the ATM receipts, which doesn't make sense. I'm not quite sure why I keep them.

SOFTWARE CONSULTANT, MALE, 36

MY WEALTHY UNCLE tries to drive on the inside of curves because he once read that on a long trip, this technique could save up to two gallons of gasoline, resulting in quite a nice chunk of money saved.

SPEECH-LANGUAGE PATHOLOGIST, FEMALE, 27

HER UNCLE: CHIROPRACTOR, MALE, 56

WHEN I EAT OUT, I always eat the most expensive part of the meal first. If I order filet mignon, for example, I will eat all of the filet mignon before I eat the side dishes. Even if the side dish is something really good that's particularly interesting or exciting, like scalloped potatoes. I feel that I want to get my money's worth by eating the steak first rather than the side dishes, which I consider to be an add-on.

BANK LOAN OFFICER, MALE, 49

I CARRY FOUR PENNIES with me at all times so I have the exact change.

DESIGNER, CHINA AND CRYSTAL, FEMALE, 24

WHEN I PAY MY MORTGAGE at the end of the month, I always round it up to the next dollar or sometimes the next five dollars. It becomes a round number and psychologically I feel like I'm paying off the mortgage a little faster, even if it's not by much.

CIVIL ENGINEER, MALE, 33

IN ADDITION to the American money in my wallet, I carry three international bills that I've collected. They are a Bulgarian lev, a French franc, and a Baghdad dinar. They're small denominations. A friend of mine who was in Baghdad gave the dinar to me. I got the Bulgarian lev when I went to Bulgaria, and since I'm French, I've been to France many times, so it was easy to get the franc. I've been doing this pretty much ever since I've had a wallet. I was a coin collector and now I guess I'm a bill collector. I never remove them from my wallet. I have no idea why I do it.

ACTOR, MALE, 31

BECAUSE HE CAN'T BEAR the thought of copper mixed in with silver, my friend throws his pennies away.

STOCKBROKER, MALE, 34

HIS FRIEND: MANAGING DIRECTOR, MALE, 35

I'M UNCOMFORTABLE about withdrawing a large sum of money from the bank because I think that I will spend it faster and I will have no money left in the bank. My solution is to withdraw a twenty-dollar bill each time even if it means going back to the bank several more times. Instead of taking out one hundred dollars, I will take out twenty dollars even though I know I will spend that twenty-dollar bill immediately and I will need more money. I think that I'm saving money by taking it out a little at a time, but I probably end up spending more money and using my credit card, which compounds the problem.

MARKETING MANAGER, TELECOMMUNICATION, MALE, 34

MY FATHER COUNTS all the money in his wallet and pocket, including the change, before going to bed. He then puts it on the night table and when he wakes up in the morning he counts it again. Sometimes when we were young, we'd take some change or a few dollars and he'd always know and be upset and he would try to find out who took it.

MANAGER, AEROSPACE ENGINEERING, FEMALE, 39
HER FATHER: PROFESSION AND AGE UNKNOWN

I NEVER KEEP MY MONEY in my wallet. I keep change and singles in my left pocket and in the right pocket, I keep fives, tens, and twenties.

FINANCE AND ACCOUNTING CONSULTANT, MALE, 49

WHEN I FIND A PENNY on the street I pick it up and always say, "Thank you," as if it were a gift from heaven. I believe that when we appreciate money that is received, the chances of getting more are increased. I have high expectations of slot machines and I thank the machine in advance. I also say "Thank you" out loud when I win money from a slot machine.

"STUDENT OF LIFE," FEMALE, 64

Every time I go by a bagpiper I hand them a dollar because you have to pay the piper. They always take it.

PRODUCER, MALE, 30

I CANNOT START my day without checking my bank account balances online. I check to see if the following items have cleared the previous day:

- ✔ ATM withdrawals
- ✔ Deposits
- ✔ Checks
- ✔ Online billpay payments
- ✔ Automatic deposits from my checking account to my brokerage account
- ✔ Automatic payments (my insurance is set to auto-matically withdraw from my checking account every month)

If I don't check, then I wonder about it all day. It's not an "I am nervous about fraud" thing—I'm just curious and I want to know!

CONSULTANT, BUSINESS PLANS FOR SMALL START-UP BUSINESSES, MALE, 29

MY COLLEAGUE THINKS it's a waste of time to balance her checkbook, so what she does is to mentally carry the sum in her head. She does that for about six months. At the end of six months, she closes the account and goes to another bank and opens up a new account. Eventually everything works out and she finds out how much money she has.

RETIRED EDUCATOR, MALE, 59

HIS FRIEND: EDUCATOR, 50

I NEVER KEEP my quarters in the same pocket as the other change. I don't really know why—maybe it's because I always seem to be looking for quarters.

COLLEGE STUDENT, MALE, 20

MY WIFE has a very special philosophy. It is: If something is free, you have to go. She wants me to go to shows, movies, and events, whatever it is as long as it's free. If it's free, even if it's poorly rated, that's better than paying to go see something that you know is going to be really good. Same with products. If she has a coupon for a product, she will go out of her way to find the product and she will buy it even if she hasn't tried it before or it's inferior. All this just to save as little as twenty-five cents instead of buying a known product that might cost a little more. That's just the way it goes.

PHYSICIAN, MALE, 45
HIS WIFE: LAWYER, 43

10¢ OFF
TODAY ONLY!

I'LL BUY SOMETHING just to get rid of a bill that's dirty so I can have cleaner money. The thought of so many people touching money turns me off.

DIAMOND DEALER, MALE, 55

WHEN I BUY A LOTTERY TICKET, I reach into my pocket for my change and if they're mostly all tails, I put the change back into my pocket and I won't rub off the lottery ticket. About a half an hour later, I'll reach into my pocket again and this time, if the change is mostly heads, I'll rub off the lottery ticket because my chances of having a winner are greater.

JR: Has this system been working for you?

Not 100 percent. I have more losing tickets in my drawer at work than winners.

PRODUCTION MANAGER, MALE, 54

AT THE ATM, although the screen says, "Thank you, it's a pleasure to serve you," and I know my session is done, I'll wait until the screen refreshes for a new user to make sure no one else can take my money.

WEB SITE PRODUCER, MALE, 28

WHEN MY GRANDFATHER was alive he would always give me twenty-five dollars or fifty dollars in singles straight from the bank so the bills were new and crisp each time. It was never in any other denomination—always ones. As a kid, it was exciting to have a big stack of money. Kids are too young to appreciate the value of money, so one fifty-dollar bill doesn't seem as much as a stack of fifty ones. My parents were cleaning out his house when he died and they found a wad of ones. They gave five crisp one-dollar bills to each of us kids in an envelope with "love, Grandpa" written on it. I keep it in my jewelry case and I will always treasure the five one-dollar bills from my grandpa.

ACCOUNT EXECUTIVE, FEMALE, 25

Assorted Nuts

"Coffee-and" has been my blight.
"Coffee-and" from morn to night
Coffee's one thing I can't stand,
I drink it merely for the "and."

I REFILL MY CUP with coffee continuously as needed in the morning until 11:30 A.M. At that time I promptly spill it out and don't have any more the rest of the day.

HOMEMAKER, FEMALE, 41

I USED TO WORK for a large Swiss bank where millions, sometimes billions, of dollars are traded. Every morning that I had Froot Loops for breakfast, something dreadful happened. I'm not kidding. All the lines in the exchange would go down or I miscalculated the dividends that we were supposed to collect on a particular date—something horrible would happen. I will not eat Froot Loops anymore for fear that something desperate will happen. I now have a food aversion—if I walk down the aisle in the supermarket and I see them, I'm like, "Ohhhhh noooooo!"

 JR: What do you have for breakfast now?

Cheerios aren't bad and Smart Start—that's got a good name. How can you go wrong by eating Smart Start? Froot Loops is kind of like a self-fulfilling prophecy.

Now that you know this about me, if you see me walking down the street, you'll think, "Oh yeah, that guy—you're not going to see him eating Froot Loops. No, sir."

CHIEF INFORMATION OFFICER, TECHNOLOGIST FOR TRADING FIRM, MALE, 38

THIS IS KIND OF WEIRD . . . When I bake a chicken and pull it out of the oven, I hurry up and cut off the little piece of white cartilage at the end of the breast bone and I eat it before anyone sees me do it. It has no flavor but I kind of crave it. I don't want anyone to see me because I think it's odd.

RETIRED, FEMALE, 52

WHEN MY HUSBAND wants to remind himself to take leftovers or fruit to the office the next day, he leaves his wallet in the refrigerator overnight. When he's about to leave the house in the morning and can't find his wallet, he'll recall that it's in the refrigerator and then he remembers to take the food with him.

HER HUSBAND: The cold wallet in my pocket is very numbing for about an hour until it warms up.

LAWYER, FEMALE, 44

HER HUSBAND: LAWYER, 44

FOR BREAKFAST EVERY MORNING, I eat marmalade straight from the jar. I do not put it on bread or have anything else other than tea with it. I am a sugar addict, and I like the high it gives me to start the day.

ARTIST/SCULPTOR, FEMALE, AGE NOT DISCLOSED

I DO SOMETHING I never noticed before until one of the checkout people at the supermarket alerted me to the fact that I do it. I sort my food by food group on the conveyer belt. You shop by food groups—first you may go through the produce section for fruits and vegetables, then on to the deli for some meat, et cetera. For some reason that's the way I sort it when I'm unloading it, fruits and vegetables, meats, breads and cereals, and so on.

RADIO PRODUCER, MALE, 32

IN COLLEGE I was not allowed to have a hot plate in my room. We were only allowed to have hot air poppers and microwave ovens. I read my lease agreement very carefully. It didn't say that I couldn't have an iron. So I turned my iron upside down and used it as a hot plate to cook food. I'm Armenian and I grew up on rice pilaf and that's what I made on it. I put books on both sides of it and then a book on top of those two stacks because the iron has an L-shaped handle. I hooked the handle over the top book. I put some cloth or something underneath it so it wouldn't wobble. Then I put a pot on it and—it's funny—the boiling water or in this case, chicken broth, had the shape of the iron as the boiling pattern because that's where the heat was. It works! You have to turn it up to "cotton" for the water to boil.

LAWYER, MALE, 36

I EAT PIZZA from the opposite end. I start with the crust on the wide part instead of biting into the point. It's something that I've been doing since I was a kid. People say, "You're weird, why do you do it that way?"

ACCOUNTANT, MALE, 31

WHEN EATING A MEAL, after two or three bites the meat is no longer warm and I find that very disturbing, so I came up with an invention to solve this problem. I remove all the handles from my frying pans and use them as plates. I keep the pan warm and when I finish cooking the steak and vegetables, I put it in the warm pan without the handle and use it as my plate. I can enjoy the steak, which stays warm until the end. Because I live alone, I can get away with this—it wouldn't work on the dining room table.

RETIRED RESTAURANT CONSULTANT, MALE, 73

THE SALAD cannot be on the same dish as the other food. I always use a separate plate for my salad. If the salad is served before the meal, I have to get rid of that plate and I must have a fresh one for my meal. If I can't have a separate plate, I won't eat the salad. If it's on the same plate, it nauseates me and I can't eat anything. It looks terrible; it doesn't go together. There's something about cold and warm . . .

PROJECT MANAGER, INTERNET, FEMALE, 41

I CANNOT DRINK CAPPUCCINO out of a glass. I can drink it out of paper; I can drink it out of ceramic; but I cannot drink it out of glass. It's hard to hold a glass cup because it's too hot. If it's served in a glass, I won't drink it.

JR: In a restaurant, do you request a different type of cup if it is served in a glass cup?

No, I don't because that's their thing and it's my problem. I give it to my husband. We won't go to certain places because they serve it in a glass.

INTERIOR DESIGNER, FEMALE, 31

My teacher would rather buy more dishes and glasses than wash the ones he already owns. He leaves them in the sink for months and then he goes out and buys new ones. I asked him why he doesn't use paper plates and cups. He said he has to use china and glass.

STUDENT, FEMALE, 20

HER TEACHER: PHYSICIAN'S ASSISTANT, 30S

WHEN I'VE DECIDED what beverage I would like to drink, I go to the cupboard and analyze the different mugs, cups, and glasses that are there. I select the shape and type of material that I think best suits the beverage on that particular day. It can change from day to day. There is no set pattern. Today I may choose a different wineglass than I did yesterday to drink the same wine because my mood may be different. It's a very strong urge each time I select a glass. To be honest, I spend time on this, sometimes several minutes, until it feels right to me.

JR: Do you feel the same way about plates?

Not to the same extent but there is a tendency.

VICE PRESIDENT, BANKING INDUSTRY, MALE, 38

Oreo cookies are not the only food that tastes good when they're dunked in milk and coffee. I will dunk virtually any food in my coffee. It can be a bagel with lox. In fact, this morning I had a cup of coffee already but I bought a bagel with cream cheese and it just looked wanting without coffee, so I took a cup and I asked my wife for part of her coffee. I didn't drink the coffee—I used the quarter cup of coffee to dunk my bagel and cream cheese in.

ATTORNEY, MALE, 39

AT THE SUPERMARKET I always begin my shopping in the produce section. I've tried starting in another aisle, but it just doesn't work for me. It's a quirk, I guess.

ACTOR, MALE, 42

WHEN EATING A MEAL, I eat half of each item on the plate in order and then I go around again and eat the other half of each item in the same order. After eating each item, I have to have a drink of milk to separate them. I eat half the meat, take a drink of milk, then half the vegetable, take a drink of milk, then half the potato, take a drink of milk, and, finally, half the bread. If for some reason I space out and skip the vegetable, the next time around I will eat half of it and throw the other half away. Two-round meals.

JR: How long has this been going on?
My entire life, basically.

RADIO HOST, MALE, 35

I DON'T HAVE A DISHWASHER, so I dry my dishes in the microwave. I set it for about a minute and a half at high and it works perfectly.

INTERNATIONAL IMPORT/EXPORT TRADER, MALE, 31

I WAS WATCHING *Jeopardy!* one day and Alex Trebek was interviewing a contestant who said that he had an unusual hobby—he collected banana stickers. I said to my wife, "I wonder how many I can collect," and I, too, began collecting banana stickers. I found a Chiquita label on a banana in the kitchen and I put it in the back of a book I was reading, which became my album. The next day I went to the supermarket and I saw bananas with a Dole label and I bought them. A few days later I was in the supermarket again and I saw a Del Monte label that I didn't have and which I wanted to add to my collection, but I didn't need the bananas, so I developed a banana sticker–swiping skill. I tore off a plastic bag in the produce department, put it in the palm of my hand and approached the bananas cautiously, using my peripheral vision to make sure no one was watching because I'm not a very competent thief, especially since I'm a parole officer and I try to abide by the law. With my forefinger and thumb, I peeled off the Del Monte sticker, palmed it into the plastic bag, and as I put the bananas back down, I discreetly slipped the bag with the banana sticker into my pocket. When I got home, I gleefully peeled it off and put it into my album. Now I had three stickers.

Since then I've collected more than seventy-five different banana stickers on the last five pages of my book. I have stickers from around the world. When friends travel overseas, they bring me back banana stickers. My neighbor's son, who is in the Peace Corps in Costa Rica, brought me back about eight or nine stickers that I had never seen before. I discovered a Web site where other collectors have their collections online and I've downloaded pages and pages of collections.

I guarantee that the next time you're in the supermarket and you see bananas, you'll think of me.

JR: There's no doubt about that.

PAROLE OFFICER, MALE, 53

I NEED TO EAT all my food in the same proportion. They can't touch and they all need to be at the same level. I'll stop eating one item of food and continue around the plate to each item while maintaining the same levels. I keep them even as I go along throughout the entire meal.

ACCOUNT MANAGER, FEMALE, 25

WHEN MY WIFE AND I share a drink, she'll drink it down to the last sip and then she'll hand it over to me. Technically, since there is a tiny amount left, she knows that I can't accuse her of finishing it and not leaving any for me even though there's not nearly enough to quench my thirst.

SOFTWARE ENGINEER, IT FIRM, MALE, 30
HIS WIFE: PROFESSION AND AGE UNKNOWN

MY KIDS, one is six and the other is almost two, can't eat their dinner if the microwave door is ajar. If either of them sees it that way, they will get up and close it before they can sit down and have their meal.

SIX-YEAR-OLD SON: I can't eat dinner because I'll just keep staring at it.

CONSULTANT, FEMALE, 44

WHENEVER I EAT small pieces of candy or food, like M&M's or peanuts, I split it up evenly inside my mouth so each side of my mouth gets an equal amount. For example, if I have three Skittles, I'll put one on one side, one on the other side and split the third one in half so there's one and one half Skittles on each side. I'll actually split an individual peanut in half. I don't like to play favorites.

ACCOUNTANT, MALE, 22

MY FRIEND WON'T EAT GRAPES if they fall off the stem because he thinks they're for peasants. He calls them "poor man's grapes." If they're not connected to the stem he just throws them away. I discovered this when we were pulling grapes off the stem and putting them in a dish so we wouldn't have to pick them off and he said he doesn't eat grapes that are picked off the stem.

DRAFTSMAN, MALE, 36
HIS FRIEND: RETIRED, 54

MY WIFE WILL NEVER eat a round cake—only square ones. I think she got it from her mother.

RADIO CALLER, MALE, PROFESSION AND AGE UNKNOWN

THERE ARE CERTAIN LIQUIDS, such as juices, that I must drink through a straw, but I absolutely cannot drink other liquids, such as water, through a straw. The straw changes the taste and texture of the drink. My girlfriend thinks I'm nuts.

SALESMAN, RETAIL, MALE, 43

MY HUSBAND HAS THIS QUIRK that drives me crazy. He fills a glass with ice, adds his drink of choice and then swirls the contents before each sip, claiming that the swirling motion cools the drink faster. He is forty-seven and has been doing it all his life, at least since he grew out of a sippy cup, but maybe even then too!

BOOKKEEPER, FEMALE, 45
HER HUSBAND: JEWELER/JEWELRY BUSINESS OWNER, 47

MY HUSBAND calls the waiter over and has him clear all the dishes after each course so the table is clean before allowing the next course to be served. If the waiter is unavailable, he'll put the dishes on an empty table. At the end of the meal, he places his napkin in front of him in lieu of a clean tablecloth. There can't be any crumbs in front of him.

FULL-TIME MOM, FEMALE, 29

HER HUSBAND: SALES MANAGER, 30S

I'VE BEEN WEARING SUNGLASSES while raiding the refrigerator almost every night for about thirty-five years. I keep a pair of sunglasses on top of the refrigerator. I put them on so the bright glare of the light doesn't disturb me when I open the refrigerator door in the middle of the night for cookies and milk.

POWER MANUFACTURER, MALE, 54

I EAT FOOD IN EVEN NUMBERS. If I have one bite of meat left on the plate, I cut it into two pieces and eat both pieces at the same time. I eat French fries in twos or fours and if there's one French fry left I take two bites of it. It's a science.

ADVERTISING MANAGER, FEMALE, 35

I LIKE EATING ICE CREAM with potato chips. I mix them together. I love the salty, soury taste mixed with the sweet. It tastes good and it's crunchy. I don't eat them separately, only together.

COLLEGE STUDENT, FEMALE, 23

I ABSOLUTELY HAVE TO SIT facing the front door in a restaurant. Recently, when I met a client for a business lunch, it seemed as though we were trying to pass each other to get to the table first. We both ended up on the same side and when I explained to him, "I have this quirk . . ." He laughed and said, "So do I!"

SALES REP, DIGITAL IMAGING SYSTEMS, MALE, 51

HIS CLIENT: PURCHASING AGENT, CORPORATION, MALE, 38

AFTER GROCERY SHOPPING, my mother would rearrange the refrigerator. The new items were put in the back and the older items were moved to the front and everything was organized so that similar items were grouped together. Sometimes she would have to remove everything to reorganize them. When she lived with us, she rearranged our refrigerator.

SOCIOLOGIST, MALE, 66

HIS MOTHER: CLAIMS EXAMINER, UNION MEDICAL BENEFITS, DECEASED

When my father wants a piece of fruit, like an apple, he'll cut it in half, eat half, put the other half in the fridge, go back and get another apple, cut that in half and only eat half of that one. The other halves eventually go bad and get thrown out.

GRADUATE STUDENT, FEMALE, 24

HER FATHER: BUSINESSMAN, 64

I LINE UP all my food by color before I start to cook. All the bright colors, such as yellow peppers and carrots, have to be arranged together on the counter and all the pastel colors, such as shallots, garlic, and small pieces of onion, get grouped together. It looks beautiful and it's as exciting visually as the taste of the food.

INVESTMENT BANKER, MALE, 51

MY LITTLE BOSTON TERRIER and I have some quiet time together every morning. Although he's perfectly capable of eating breakfast by himself from his bowl, he sits on my lap and eats his breakfast from his own special little spoon. Now he won't eat it any other way.

RETIRED, FEMALE, 52

MY MOTHER IS OBSESSIVE about having ice in her drink. She even puts ice in her tea and in her milk. She always has to have a cup completely loaded with ice. In a restaurant, Mother will order her drink and a cup of ice. She's a very skinny, slightly built woman who is always cold, but she must have ice in her drinks.

JR: Does she ever have a hot beverage?
I don't think so.

MANAGER, AEROSPACE ENGINEERING, FEMALE, 39
HER MOTHER: RETIRED SECRETARY, 62

I MUST EAT THINGS on my plate clockwise. I start at the top left and eat whatever item is there first and continue clockwise, finishing each item before I eat the next one.

GRAPHIC DESIGNER, FEMALE, 20s

WHEN I EAT MY CEREAL in the morning, I have to eat it in such a way that I have equal amounts of milk and cereal on every spoonful and when I finish the last spoonful, there's no extra milk or flakes left in the bowl. I finish them simultaneously.

JR: Can you always accurately judge the proportions?
Every single time.

ARTIST, FEMALE, 31

I ALWAYS RUN the microwave in multiples of twelve seconds. It has to do with twelve being my favorite number. Twelve months; twelve apostles; twelve hours; twelve donuts; twelve-step programs; twelve days of Christmas. It has always surprised me that in a base-ten world, so many things shake out in twelves.

MBA STUDENT, MALE, 26

SOMETIMES, when I go grocery shopping, I pick a letter of the alphabet and buy only items starting with that letter. I love a good C-shopping day:

> Carrots
> Chocolate chips
> Cauliflower
> Cow milk
> Corn
> Creamy creations
> Coffee
> Chops, pork
> Chorizo

Some products can be problematic. If I need beer or steak, and it's my C-day, I've got to switch to Spanish and add cerveza and carne to my list.

When I invite the kids across the street for supper, I let them pick a letter (some letters are off limits). Our favorite has been the P Party (pizza, punch, pineapple, Popsicles).

C is definitely the most common letter. Just this week I bought cat food, cantaloupe, and cream, iced. (Ice cream was on sale, so I had to work it in.)

At holidays, I shop by colors. For Valentine's Day I only buy red food.

I became aware of this shopping quirk about ten years ago when I noticed that everything on a particular grocery list began with the letter C. Then I began to make my lists according to letters. C is still the predominant letter for me. I don't shop by letters every single time, but since I love grocery stores and I go grocery shopping multiple times each week, it's easy for me to pick up a few things that begin with one letter.

 JR: Do people notice? Do you get interesting comments?

The clerks never notice. I point it out to them occasionally. Sometimes they get in the spirit of my shopping; other times they just ring up the stuff without any interest.

RACONTEUR, FEMALE, 57

OUR COLLEAGUE at work eats the same sandwich every single day. It's the same chicken sandwich from the same fast-food grilled chicken place with the same dressing, same fries, and the same club soda beverage. This has been his lunch for the four years that I've worked there and probably long before.

ENGINEER FOR STRUCTURAL ARCHITECTS, MALE, 30

HIS FRIEND: ARCHITECT, MALE, 45

I ALWAYS TAKE SIPS from the water fountain in multiples of four. I think I just like the rhythm of four sips at a time. Four sips is a good drink when you stop at a water fountain in the hallway, and eight or twelve work well after exercise.

MBA STUDENT, MALE, 26

MY WIFE arranges all her spices in alphabetical order. When I look for a particular spice, I can never find it, so I rearrange it based on color. She changes it back and we start the whole thing all over again.

DIRECTOR OF MARKETING, TEXTILE COMPANY, MALE, 30

HIS WIFE: CLOTHING DESIGNER, 30

I CAN ONLY HAVE one item of food on my plate. During meals, after I finish the main dish, I will wash my plate with soap and water. Then I will have a side dish, wash the plate again, and so on until I finish all the food. More specifically, first I'll eat the meat, then I will clean the plate, then I'll have the vegetables, clean the plate, then the salad, and clean the plate. It just doesn't taste good when they're mixed together. In a restaurant, I ask them to put everything on separate plates.

JR: Why don't you put each food on a separate plate and have it on the table at the same time?

Then it's more work for my mom.

COLLEGE JUNIOR, MALE, 21

I WON'T FINISH the last sip of a drink. I will leave it unfinished or I will spill it out and refill my glass. I don't like the fact that it has been sitting there the longest.

BROADCAST TRAFFIC COORDINATOR, FEMALE, 28

I EAT FROM THE RIGHT SIDE of the plate to the left side of the plate in a nice orderly fashion. I begin with whatever food is on the right when it is placed in front of me.

JR: Do you have any idea why you do this?
I'm crazy.

REAL ESTATE FINANCE ANALYST, MALE, 30

For breakfast every morning, I have cereal in my coffee. Occasionally I'll have a muffin, and that goes into the coffee as well. It's like a soup. Coffee, sugar, milk, and cereal in the coffee cup.

DIRECTOR, LEARNING CENTER, FEMALE, 35

I PREFER TO DRINK my coffee out of a paper cup. Coffee tastes better in a paper cup. Even when I am eating on the premises in a coffee shop, I request a paper cup. If my request is refused and I am told that they can only serve coffee in a ceramic cup, I leave the restaurant and go somewhere else.

PRESIDENT, TEXTILE COMPANY, MALE, 58

ANYTIME I BARBECUE, I always have to have a hot dog first before I eat anything else because I love hot dogs. That's a ritual of mine. No matter what I'm making I always, always must have a hot dog first.

ENVELOPE MANUFACTURER, MALE, 42

I NEED TO GET at least four Cheerios on the spoon at the same time. If I get just one or two, I have to fish around until it's at least four. It could be more than four but four is the minimum. Four fits nicely on the spoon. One or two just doesn't look right.

ACCOUNTANT, MALE, 27

I EAT CHEESEBURGERS from the outside in a circular fashion until I get to the middle, which is the best part. The middle is the perfect piece where every bit of what makes up a cheeseburger—the burger, the cheese, the ketchup, and the onions—has come together. It is saved for last.

ASSOCIATE MARKETING MANAGER, FEMALE, 24

MY WIFE AND I used to argue over who gets to pour the hot water in our kettle first. We now have two separate kettles to boil water and two toasters in separate areas of the kitchen so we won't fight over who goes first. I have a toaster oven and a kettle and she has a regular toaster and a kettle.

DIRECTOR, PUBLIC FOUNDATION AND INVESTOR, MALE, 53

AFTER I EAT A MEAL, I leave the glass with my beverage on the table and take a different glass even if I continue drinking the same beverage. I don't like to see food residue on the glass once I'm finished eating. It just doesn't look appealing.

HOTEL DEVELOPER, MALE, 32

I EAT EVERYTHING with a fork and knife, even corn on the cob, pizza, and chicken wings. It started when I wore braces on my teeth. I didn't want to bite into something and have food stick to my braces, so I cut it up and put it in the back of my mouth. To this day I still do it that way. It drives people crazy.

COMMUNICATIONS CONSULTANT, MALE, 50

MY MOTHER orders salad with blue cheese dressing and Thousand Island dressing, both on the side. She has to have both and eats the salad using both dressings.

ACADEMIC ADMINISTRATOR, MALE, 29

HIS MOTHER: ADMINISTRATIVE ASSISTANT, BIOTECH INDUSTRY, 50s

I CAN'T HAVE what I call serious foods with sweet foods. They're separate categories. I can't have pineapple or fruit or anything of that sort on what's supposed to be serious food. For breakfast, I need to have my syrup and pancakes on one plate and my hash browns and bacon on a completely different plate. I don't like it when they all mix together.

ENROLLMENT COORDINATOR, MARKETING, FEMALE, 24

I crumble desserts, completely smash them, and only then do I eat them. It feels like there's more of it.

PERMISSIONS COORDINATOR, MAGAZINE PUBLISHER, FEMALE, 24

I ALWAYS USE a dessert fork instead of a spoon when I make tea. I developed this habit at my last job, which, for some reason, was short on spoons in the kitchen. There were two or three spoons, and by the time everyone had coffee, there were no clean ones left. So I got in the habit of using the small dessert forks, which were available in abundance, and now that's all I ever use.

I have a whole little tea bag routine (I guess most tea drinkers do), and I prefer the fork because it turns out it's a better tool for my particular routine. First, I use the fork to hold the bag in the bottom of the cup for a minute or two while it steeps, then I use it to swish the bag around. I have to be careful at the swishing stage not to tear open the bag, but I guess I'm just used to that now. In fact, because the prongs grab onto the bag, I feel I can swirl the bag more vigorously with a fork than I can with a spoon, which makes my tea stronger faster. Then I make sure I extract all the tea goodness from the bag by folding and squeezing the bag on the fork. The spoon is harder to press against, being concave. The fork's prongs are good at forcing the last bit of liquid out, which then drains right through them. Sometimes if the bag is too hot to squeeze, but I don't want the tea to steep any longer (it gets bitter), I balance the fork across the top of the cup and rest the tea bag on it to cool. Spoons won't balance that way, but I can make most dessert forks stay put.

I'm sure that proper English ladies would be terribly outraged by this whole procedure!

DECORATIVE PILLOW DESIGNER, FEMALE, 33

ALL FOOD ITEMS have to be placed in their own categories in the pantry. Corn on top of corn, veggies on top of veggies, soups on top of soups, fruits and jellies on top of fruits and jellies. My wife, however, mixes everything up.

ELECTRICIAN, MALE, 52

HIS WIFE: TEACHER, 50

IF I'M AWARE that the tuna fish has onions chopped into it, I won't eat it, but if the onions are on top of the tuna fish, I can eat it. The same with sardines. Maybe it's the crunchiness . . . I don't know.

RESTAURATEUR, MALE, 58

AS MUCH AS I LIKE SWEETS, the one type of dessert or breakfast pastry that I would never buy or choose is jam-filled pastry. If it has jam in it, I don't want it. So I don't quite understand why, when I have a plain croissant for breakfast, I like it with jam on the side and I spread some jam on every bite. It seems like a contradiction. Maybe it's the whole ritual of applying the jam—I don't know—I haven't been able to come up with an adequate explanation to myself.

WRITER, FEMALE, 51

I eat corn in alternate rows. I eat a row and leave a row, eat another row and leave a row until 50 percent of the corn is eaten and then I twirl it around like a barber's pole.

PAROLE OFFICER, MALE, 53

WHEN I MAKE WHIPPED CREAM, I whisk it by hand versus using a machine. You can use a mixer and make a lot of noise clanging against the side of the bowl or you can do it by hand. It's much more satisfying and purer by hand and takes about the same amount of time as with a machine.

INSURANCE UNDERWRITER, MALE, 38

I EAT ALL THE GREEN VEGETABLES on my plate before any other item because I can't stand the color green.

TENNIS PRO, MALE, 23

I GRAB A CUP from the highest pile when I get my coffee at the deli across the street from my office in the morning. And as I grab it I wish myself good luck.

JR: Why do you grab it from the highest pile?

I'm reaching for higher things; it's good luck.

PARALEGAL, MALE, 30

MY FRIEND insists on eating all courses in a meal at the same time. There can only be one course. He won't have salad on a salad plate, then wait for someone to serve the main course. He eats everything, only all at the same time and on the same plate, with the exception of soup. When we invite him for dinner, depending on how many people we invite over, we'll try to serve everything together just to accommodate him because we know how irate he gets sitting and waiting while the rest of us eat the salad.

ADVERTISING EXECUTIVE, MALE, 27

HIS FRIEND: IN FINANCE, 28

I LINE UP THE ZITI in a row before I eat it. I put eight or ten in a row each time before I eat it. I feel that since I'm so disorderly in my mind, I need some order when I'm eating.

PAINTER (ARTIST), MALE, 63

MY WIFE AND I have been married for seventeen years. We established a rule that we've been following since the first day of our marriage. We must have wine with dinner. There are no exceptions to this ritual. If the cellar is empty, we eat out.

ENVELOPE MANUFACTURER, MALE, 42

HIS WIFE: HOMEMAKER, 41

I DRINK COFFEE through a straw in any situation where I'm in motion and could spill the drink on myself, such as when I'm on the train or driving my car. I also think that I get more of a burst of caffeine drinking coffee through a straw. I've been doing this for over ten years. I used to spill drinks on myself on the train and I finally said, "I can't do this anymore—I have to start using a straw." I find that those lids don't work; I still spill it on myself. Sometimes I won't even buy the coffee if they don't have straws. I've only met one other person who drinks coffee through a straw. People occasionally approach me and say, "Hot coffee will melt the straw!" It's never melted and it doesn't have the taste of plastic.

MARKETING MANAGER, TELECOMMUNICATIONS, MALE, 34

I EAT DESSERTS with the smallest spoon that I can find so it lasts longer. For example, I eat trifle (I'm from England) with a small spoon.

REALTOR, MALE, 23

IF I DIP my Oreos into milk, once the Oreos are gone I can't drink the milk with the floaties in it no matter how much milk is left.

JR: What about while you're eating the cookie?

No problem. But once I'm done with the Oreos and they're floating in there, I just can't do it.

RADIO HOST, MALE, AGE UNKNOWN

WHENEVER I MAKE TOAST, I always make four pieces. I always cover two slices with strawberry preserves as well as half of a third slice. I eat them in the following order: a jelly piece, the plain piece, the other jelly piece, and finally the piece that's half jelly and half plain. On the final piece, I eat the jelly half before the plain half. Four slices is the most bread that will fit in my toaster oven. I think I settled on two and a half slices of jelly just because it seemed like the right amount. I like both jellied and plain, and that just seemed like the perfect compromise.

MBA STUDENT, MALE, 26

MY WIFE doesn't eat vegetables. If vegetables are served on her plate along with chicken, she'll cut away the piece of chicken that touched the vegetables and she won't eat that piece.

HOTEL DEVELOPER, MALE, 32
HIS WIFE: TRAVEL WRITER, 32

My mother-in-law washes potatoes before she peels them. For what reason, I have no idea.

GRAPHIC DESIGNER, MALE, 51
HIS MOTHER-IN-LAW: RETIRED, LATE 60s–EARLY 70s

MY MOTHER ALPHABETIZES the silverware in the silverware drawer. Butter knives in the first slot, then forks, then knives, then spoons. It's weird—she's very anal about that. She gets annoyed if someone puts a utensil in the wrong place. She'll look in the drawer after I've done the dishes to make sure I put everything back in the right place.

FREELANCE PRODUCER, MALE, 28

HIS MOM: RETIRED, 68

WHEN I EAT FRENCH FRIES, I always leave one end—the tip of each fry—because it's unappealing. Everyone always laughs at me.

ASSISTANT EDITOR, MALE, 21

MY AUNT CAN'T GO to a family function or party without taking some food home to "her husband" or "for tomorrow." She does this before people at the function have eaten. Sometimes she is told to wait to see if there is anything left over (she always asks first), but it is still annoying to family members. She will usually ask for some kind of wrapper from the host/hostess of the function.

LEGAL SECRETARY, FEMALE, 44

HER AUNT: RETIRED, 68

MY HUSBAND leaves the remaining little bitty bit of food in a can or jar and then puts it back in the fridge even though he could easily finish it. This is his "clever" tactic to avoid having to wash it. It has to be washed before it's placed into the recycling bin in our building. Although he knows that I'm on to his strategy, it doesn't help. He continues to do it, confident that eventually I will wash it.

WRITER, FEMALE, 51

HER HUSBAND: ATTORNEY, 56

I ALWAYS TASTE the meat first. That's my favorite. If the meat is good, the meal is good. If the meat's not good, the meal's not good.

REPORTER, MALE, 58

EVERY MORNING I add a teaspoon of water to my coffee because I can't drink it until I cool it off a little bit, even though the coffee may not be too hot to drink. It's as though I'm anointing my coffee. A cube of ice is okay, but generally I prefer a little bit of water.

RADIO PRODUCER, MALE, MID- TO LATE 30S

I ABSOLUTELY MUST sample the cheesecake in every restaurant that I go to, even if I just have one bite and leave the rest. In fact, I had to give up Chinese restaurants because they don't serve cheesecake.

COPYWRITER, FEMALE, 25

MY GRANDMOTHER used to make the most delectable spinach pie. Not only was it a delicious treat but it also brought me good luck whenever I ate it, so I ate it before all my big tests. When I went away to medical school, she would send it to me. I shared it with a few close friends in my class. They looked forward to the packages of spinach pie I received almost as much as I did!

JR: Do you still eat spinach pie?

Absolutely—look how lucky I am!

GYNECOLOGIST, FEMALE, 54

AT A DINNER TABLE I must remove my plates when I'm finished eating even if other people are still eating. I put them in the sink, out of my sight. If I'm required to go back to the dinner table to socialize, then I don't wash them immediately.

 JR: Do other people feel pressured to eat more quickly?
Absolutely, but that's not my intention. After I'm finished eating, I don't want to see food.

PROGRAMMER, MALE, 30

I HATE WOODEN SPOONS. I cannot touch them. If I am emptying the dishwasher and I touch one, I have to leave the kitchen for a couple of minutes and try to forget about it. The feel of them freaks me out!

CONSULTANT, BUSINESS PLANS FOR SMALL START-UP BUSINESSES, MALE, 29

WHEN I HAVE A CUP of coffee and a banana, I always like to finish with two sips of cold coffee. That's my breakfast almost every morning. Coffee and a banana followed by the last two sips of cold coffee.

 JR: Do you always have a banana with your coffee?
Yes, I think it's absolutely the right taste combination.

INVESTMENT BANKER, MALE, 51

WHEN MY HUSBAND DRINKS any beverages or liquids, he always has to say, "Ahhhhhh." I ask him, "Why do you have to moan afterward? Just enjoy it." But he always says, "Ahhhhhhhh."

CLERK, FEMALE, 46
HER HUSBAND: LABORER, 45

I HATE WHEN GRAVY touches any of the side dishes, so what I do is take a napkin, fold it several times and prop the plate up with it. The plate stays tilted and keeps the gravy in one spot so it doesn't mix with the rice or the string beans.

ACCOUNT SPECIALIST, PUBLIC RELATIONS, MALE, 25

If I'm eating an entrée and it has rice with it, I have to finish every single grain of rice. I never even noticed it but friends would say to me, "Stop, you're chasing that one piece of rice on your plate!"

PRODUCER, ADVERTISING, MALE, 28

I EAT MY CEREAL DRY and have the milk on the side because I don't like to mix things. I don't put the cereal in my mouth and then pour some milk in. I swallow some cereal and then take a swig of milk to wash it down. Sometimes I don't use milk; sometimes I use Coca-Cola. Cheerios and Coca-Cola.

RADIO HOST, MALE, 35

I'VE NOTICED that when I'm served a plate of food, whether it's in a restaurant or at home, I have to move the plate slightly—it could be as little as a quarter of an inch—even if it was perfectly situated in front of me. I've observed other people doing the same thing.

RADIO CALLER, FEMALE, PROFESSION AND AGE UNKNOWN

WHEN MY HUSBAND was in a fraternity, he would put something disgusting on part of his food so no one else would touch it. For example, he'd put some cigarette ashes on part of a slice of pizza. It was contaminated just enough so that other people wouldn't find it appetizing anymore. He would eat around that area and the pizza remained exclusively his. He marks his territory.

ATTORNEY, FEMALE, 31
HER HUSBAND: CORPORATE ATTORNEY, 32

THE TWO SLICES OF BREAD have to match up for my sandwich to be correct. I like when my slices are neat and even.

 JR: What if two even slices are not available?

I will have an open-face sandwich.

FABRIC MERCHANDISING, FEMALE, 22

MY BEVERAGES frequently spill out of the glass or cup because I pour it all the way up to the rim. You can imagine what a hit this is with my wife! Now that I'm thinking about it, an explanation comes to mind. When we were children, whenever my mother gave us a glass of tea or any other drink, she would pour it up to the top and say, in Yiddish, "I pour this tea with my full heart."

PRIVATE INVESTOR, MALE, 61

Night Shtick

We sleep in a bed,
That's so comfy and wide,
But one problem we have,
We both want the same side.

THE FLOWER PATTERN on the comforter has to be positioned so the flowers are pointed toward the head of the bed and the stems are toward the foot of the bed, because flowers grow upward. The head of the bed is up. You don't see flowers growing down. My girlfriend disregards this logic totally.

PROJECT SUPERVISOR, CONSTRUCTION COMPANY, MALE, 40

HIS GIRLFRIEND: MAGAZINE EDITOR/NOVELIST, 38

I SET MY ALARM to an odd and uncommon number like 8:19 or 8:57. It can't be a common number like 8:15 or 8:45. I don't know why I decided to set my clock to an odd number, but I've been doing it for as long as I can remember. In fact, if the clock is not on an odd number I cannot sleep, that's how much it bothers me. I set my alarm clock to various times because I get up at different times. It doesn't matter what time I set it to as long as it's an odd and uncommon number. I will sit in front of the VCR clock until it says 3:47 instead of just leaving at 3:45. A couple of times it has made me late for work!

COLLEGE STUDENT, FEMALE, 19

EVERY NIGHT I have to make the bed before I go to sleep. I don't make it in the morning because I don't use it until the night. I don't sleep as well if I don't make it.

PHYSICIAN, MALE, 34

WHEN I GO TO SLEEP EVERY NIGHT, I sleep on a soft pillow and a hard pillow. I put the hard pillow in the back and the soft pillow in the front and I cannot go to sleep unless the openings of the pillowcases are facing toward the outside of the bed. If they're inside, it's bad luck and I can't go to sleep.

HOMEMAKER, FEMALE, 41

I CAN'T START THE DAY without making my bed in the morning. If for some reason it's unmade, I can't go to bed at night without first making the bed. If I'm in a hotel even though I know the housekeeper is coming and she will make it, at the very least, I have to pull the covers up so it's not a mess while I'm getting dressed.

TEACHER, FEMALE, 31

I MUST RUB MY FEET TOGETHER to fall asleep. One foot is under the sheets and the other foot is over the sheets—it's just so relaxing and comforting. I've been doing this since I was a little girl.

LEGAL ASSISTANT, FEMALE, 43

MY MOTHER ALWAYS TOLD ME to go out of the house with my right foot first on the day of a big event such as the first day of school or the first day of a job. I've taken this "a step" further. I have to get out of my bed with my right foot first every morning because then I am assured of having good luck for the entire day. This is not so easily accomplished because I sleep on the left side of the bed so sometimes it requires an acrobatic act to get my right foot out first.

OWNER, CHILDCARE BUSINESS, FEMALE, 46

AS SOON AS I GET HOME FROM WORK, I automatically get into my pajamas before I do anything around the house. I get home at about 7:30 P.M., change, and stay in my pajamas.

DISPLAY DEVELOPMENT, FEMALE, 31

EVEN THOUGH I'M FIFTY-FIVE YEARS OLD, I always hold onto at least one stuffed animal when I sleep. When we travel I take a stuffed animal with me. It's usually Panda because he's little. Occasionally I will forget to bring a stuffed animal with me and then we have to rush out wherever we are and find a stuffed animal. When I leave Panda behind and travel with a different stuffed animal, I feel guilty. Or if I take Panda with me and then put him on the shelf when I come home and sleep with Teddy Eddie, I still feel guilty. I'm really weirder than I thought!

JR: When one of the stuffed animals becomes old and worn, do you throw it out?

Rarely, but it just so happens that a very old little teddy bear that I sleep with in our summer bungalow got badly mutilated over the winter—the moths must have gotten him. I threw him in the garbage and, to tell you the truth, I felt guilty. I know it's not rational because these animals are just pieces of cloth and buttons and thread, but they've been part of the family.

REHABILITATION COUNSELOR, FEMALE, 55

MY HANDS GET DRY, so before I go to bed I use moisturizer and then put on ski gloves, which I sleep in. I take them off when I get up in the morning. Ski gloves are the only kind of gloves I have. I no longer ski, so they're my hand gloves now.

TELEVISION PRODUCER, MALE, 29

MY BEDSHEETS have to be ironed. I'm incapable of sleeping on wrinkled sheets. The wrinkles bother me; I can feel them on my skin. I wash and iron the sheets and pillowcases every ten days. Ironing them is a tough job because I live in a small apartment. My shirts are dry-cleaned and pressed. The rest of my laundry is done at the Laundromat.

BANKER, MALE, 28

I CAN'T FACE THE WALL when I'm sleeping, because I think somebody's going to be behind me on the other side. I need to always face away from the wall.

STUDENT, MALE, 13

BEFORE GOING TO BED I have a 7UP float. It's composed of skim milk, chocolate syrup, 7UP, and some ice cream. It started about thirty years ago. My wife brings the ingredients on vacation with us or we buy the items when we get there.

MANAGER, SIGN MANUFACTURING COMPANY, MALE, 53

AFTER 11 P.M., if the lights are off, I won't go back out into the rest of the house because I'm scared. If I'm in my bed and the lights are on, then I'm not afraid. If it's dark, then I don't like getting out of my bed.

VICE PRESIDENT, CORPORATE COMMUNICATIONS, FEMALE, 29

IN ORDER FOR ME to effectively fall asleep, the side of my bed has to be against the wall. If I'm traveling or away from home somewhere, I move the bed against the wall.

ART AND MUSEUM ADMINISTRATOR, MALE, 24

FROM DAY ONE, since I began wearing makeup at the age of fourteen, I've gone to bed with my makeup on. I brush my teeth before going to bed but I'm not motivated enough and just too tired at night to remove my makeup. I've gotten all kinds of dire predictions of how this will affect my face but makeup has lanolin in it, which is actually very good for skin. So here I am doing the right thing for the wrong reasons.

JR: Do your sheets get dirty?

I sleep mostly on my back or side and I don't buy light-colored linen. I keep hoping Paul Newman will appear in a dream and if he does, I want to look good.

RETIRED GUIDANCE COUNSELOR/ACTRESS, FEMALE, 70s

WHEN I GO TO SLEEP my feet have to be really clean. If I come home late at night, I take a "feet bath." It's very uncomfortable for me to get into bed with my feet dirty. I don't care about my hands or hair—I just need my feet to be clean. I'm weird.

STOCKBROKER, MALE, 37

To make sure she wakes up on time, my wife sets four alarm clocks, all set to ring at the same time. She used to work in the airline industry, maybe that's where it started. If she gets up and leaves early, sometimes she doesn't remember to turn them all off.

ATTORNEY, MALE, 45

HIS WIFE: OCCUPATIONAL THERAPIST, HEALTH CARE INDUSTRY, 30s

IN MY BEDROOM at my parents' house, I have four glow-in-the-dark stars on my wall. From the time I got them when I was thirteen until I moved out of my parents' house, every night when I went to bed and the lights were out, I would look over my left shoulder and say good luck to the stars. Then I'd roll over, look over my right shoulder and say good luck to the stars again. Only then could I go to sleep. If, for any reason I got out of bed, for a glass of water or to go to the bathroom, I'd have to repeat the entire process. When I visit my parents and stay in my room, I still go through this ritual. I can't fall asleep otherwise. It will bother me until I do it.

PRODUCTION ASSISTANT, MALE, 25

Good luck!

Good luck!

BEFORE I GO TO SLEEP I listen to the radio, but I can't turn it off in the middle of a song. I have to wait until it ends. If I'm a little slow and another song begins, I have to finish listening to that one.

STUDENT, FEMALE, 13

I CANNOT SLEEP with both legs under the covers. One leg must be out. I can regulate how hot or cold I am by moving my legs in and out of the covers.

REAL ESTATE CONSULTANT, MALE, 24

I ALWAYS HAVE TO HAVE ONE LEG above the comforter. I cannot sleep completely underneath the blankets. It's a "cuddling" thing—I need to cuddle with the comforter.

CONSULTANT, BUSINESS PLANS FOR SMALL START-UP BUSINESSES, MALE, 29

SOMETIMES I'M JUST TOO TIRED to remove my clothes at night. I put my head down on the pillow and instead of waking up an hour later, I sleep through the night. When I wake up in the morning, I find that I'm fully clothed in my street clothes from the day before. I take a shower, change my underwear and if the clothes I slept in are not too badly wrinkled, I wear them again that day. Clothes that are permanent press don't get that wrinkled.

JR: Do you wear them to work or just on the weekend?
Both. My office is informal.

JR: How many times do you wear the same clothes?
If I've slept in them, I'll only wear them again the day after.

JR: Do you wear your shoes to bed?
No.

JR: How does your wife feel about this?
She doesn't approve.

ACCOUNTANT, MALE, 52

I sleep with one leg out of the covers and none of my sheets can be tucked in. I don't like feeling trapped under the covers. I think this must be common because I learned that my dad does it also.

BROADCAST TRAFFIC COORDINATOR, FEMALE, 28

WHEN I'M SLEEPING, the pillow, comforter, or sheets has to be between my legs so my knees don't touch. I just can't stand the feeling of my knees touching each other while I'm sleeping.

SALESMAN, CATERING, MALE, 33

IF I'M READING a scary book before I go to bed, I have to move the book out of my bedroom into another room in the house before I can go to sleep. I'm afraid that the characters will come out and attack me in the middle of the night.

COLLEGE STUDENT, FEMALE, 21

AT NIGHT, no matter how late I get home or how tired I am, I can't just plop into bed. I go through a ritual I call "Passing Water," which is a therapeutic shower without soap. I just let the water run over me. The warm water is relaxing and soothing. I take a regular shower with soap in the morning. Anyone who is with me is required to take a "Passing Water" shower as well.

GRAPHIC DESIGNER, MALE, 52

I HAVE TONS OF WADS OF GUM that I've stuck onto my bed-side table because when I want to go to sleep, the easiest thing is to remove the gum and stick it on the night table. In the morning I often pick up the gum and put it back in my mouth.

COLLEGE STUDENT, FEMALE, 21

WHEN I WAS A CHILD, I felt that any toys near my bed would feel lonely at night if they were far apart, so if there were two toys, I would position them so they were touching. This would enable them to have companionship at night. For the same reason, when I took my shoes off, I arranged them symmetrically so the toes and heels were aligned and touching—one shoe couldn't be forward of the other. The pair of shoes would spend the night together and be assured of not being lonely. I must confess that even as an adult, I still do that occasionally with my shoes.

COMPUTER PROGRAMMER, MALE, 60

I CAN'T HELP IT, right before I go to sleep, I have to get every last little pee out, so I go to the bathroom the second before I go to sleep.

SENIOR VICE PRESIDENT, LICENSING, FEMALE, 40

I TRAVEL QUITE A BIT and when I do I have to bring all my own bedding because I don't like the smell of sheets that are not mine. Whether I'm traveling locally for just two nights or overseas, I wash a fresh set of bed sheets and carry it around with me in an enormous duffel bag.

DIRECTOR, PUBLIC FOUNDATION AND INVESTOR, MALE, 53

I CAN BE TURNED TOWARD someone's back or I can face a wall but I cannot face someone who is facing me and sleep at the same time. I just have a hard time breathing when I have someone's face right there. If I wake up in the middle of the night and discover that I am turned toward someone's face, I must flip over or nudge them out of the way.

REAL ESTATE CONSULTANT, MALE, 24

I SET MY CLOCK in my bedroom to a different time every day, always well in advance of when I really have to get up. Today it was about twenty-four minutes early, tomorrow it may be an hour and forty minutes early. When it goes off in the morning and I think, "Oh my gosh, I've gotta get up," I then realize, "Well, I really have some extra time here." Then I have to calculate exactly how much extra time I have, so it gets my brain working. I always set it in advance so I think I'm getting something.

ACCOUNT EXECUTIVE, INSURANCE, FEMALE, 45

MY GIRLFRIEND won't sleep in a bed unless the tag of the blanket is in the right corner at the foot of the bed. It drives me nuts.

LEGAL ASSISTANT, MALE, 25

HIS GIRLFRIEND: TEACHER, 24

EVERY NIGHT before I go to bed I check behind every conceivable thing that someone could possibly hide behind—curtains, cabinets, behind the door, under my bed, under my duvet, everywhere—just in case someone is hiding.

COLLEGE STUDENT, FEMALE, 21

WHEN I GO TO SLEEP I have to have a fan on—not because I'm warm, but for the sound. If I go away somewhere and there is complete silence, it's difficult for me to fall asleep. It probably began when I went away to college four years ago. There was a lot of noise outside—music, conversation, et cetera—and when I turned on the fan, the sound of the fan blocked the street noise. In hotels, when I turn on the air conditioner in the room, it makes a similar sound.

COLLEGE STUDENT, FEMALE, 21

DURING THE SUMMER, I sleep on top of all the sheets with just a duvet pulled over me so I don't have to remake the bed in the morning and tuck everything in again with hospital corners.

PRODUCT DEVELOPER, WOMEN'S WEAR, MALE, 40

I HAVE THREE PILLOWS—two with beige pillowcases and one with a blue pillowcase. They're always stacked the same way every night. The beige ones are arranged next to each other butting at the short side. The blue one is centered on top of them. If I wake up in the middle of the night and they've shifted, I have to rearrange it or I can't fall back to sleep.

PRODUCTION ASSISTANT, MALE, 25

I HAVE TO REMOVE any ticking clock from the bedroom in order to fall asleep. I will go to any means—unscrew it if necessary—or remove the clock from the room so I don't hear that *tick . . . tick . . . tick*. It's like Captain Hook and that alligator—I can't do it.

ASSOCIATE ACCOUNTANT, MALE, 23

When we go to a hotel, my wife has to make the bed before we leave so it looks neat and proper.

SALESMAN, PRINTING AND GRAPHICS, MALE, 34
HIS WIFE: STAY-AT-HOME MOM, 34

MY FIANCÉE SLEEPS diagonally in the bed. She doesn't want her head to be at the top of the bed or her feet to be at the bottom. When she sleeps diagonally she has the maximum amount of room around her feet and head, but there's no room for me! So when I'm ready to go to bed, I have to wake her up and move her over a little bit. Even though she knows it's coming I still have to do it every night. Then, once I'm in the bed, she starts rolling up the covers. It's like a roller—she'll flatten down one side and start rolling, so pretty soon I'm coverless and I have to wake her up again and pull the covers out.

GRAPHIC DESIGNER, MALE, 30

HIS FIANCÉE: TEMP, INTERNET COMPANY, 29

MY GIRLFRIEND props a pillow along the headboard or wall widthwise. Her head never makes contact with it when she sleeps, nor does her hair. It is simply there as a monument. If you try to take it you'll be yelled at.

SELF-EMPLOYED, REAL ESTATE, MALE, 32

HIS GIRLFRIEND: ACCOUNT EXECUTIVE, PUBLIC RELATIONS, AND ACTRESS, 31

WHEN I GO TO BED, I don't take my watch off until I'm actually under the sheets. That is when I feel that time will stop and that is my relaxation period. Otherwise time is always going.

NATIONAL SALES MANAGER, NEWSPAPER PUBLISHER, MALE, 26

EVERY THREE MONTHS I have to change my sleeping direction. If my head is at the headboard for three months, I will then sleep so my feet are at the headboard for the next three months. After a while the same position gets to be uncomfortable, so I switch. I've been doing this since I was ten.

STUDENT, COLLEGE SOPHOMORE, MALE, 19

I SLEEP IN A TENT in my backyard. It's more comfortable, the ground is soft, and, more importantly, I don't have to wake up in the morning to let the dog out. I can just unzip the zipper right next to me, roll over, and go back to sleep. I live in Alabama where it's warm all year round.

STUDENT, MALE, 22

IF I TAKE A NAP, I *cannot* do it in my bed. It *must* be on the couch. *Must. Must. Must.*

 JR: Why?

Because to me, the bed is for sleeping overnight. The couch is made for sleeping during the day.

CONSULTANT, BUSINESS PLANS FOR SMALL START-UP BUSINESSES, MALE, 29

MY FATHER will not sleep until all the clocks in the bedroom are covered. Knowing the time after he's gone to bed makes him nervous. If he wakes up and sees what time it is, he'll be anxious that he's not sleeping well or that he'll have to get up soon. He throws a sheet or a towel or a T-shirt over all the clocks every night and removes the covers in the morning.

 JR: Does he wear a watch during the day?

Yes.

COMEDIAN, MALE, 30

HIS FATHER: EDUCATIONAL CONSULTANT, 60

I HAVE FIVE PILLOWS on the bed. I arrange them in two layers. There are three pillows on the bottom layer butting each other horizontally and two pillows, also butting, centered above them. My head has to be right in the middle of the two top pillows to block out any sound around me. It works well.

BUSINESS DEVELOPMENT MANAGER, MALE, 30

I ALWAYS THROW my hair up and over the pillow. It gives my hair a nice fluff in the morning versus having a flat head. I don't change positions. I'm pretty stable.

BANK ANALYST, FEMALE, MID-30s

IN COLLEGE, when I would study I'd put my notes under my pillow so that it would sink in overnight by osmosis.

 JR: Did it?

It did! It worked—4.0 average. Even now when I have a presentation, I put the material under my pillow. It just makes me feel better.

HUMAN RESOURCES MANAGER, FEMALE, 36

MY CLOSET DOOR has to be closed when I go to sleep, otherwise I can't sleep. If I see that it's open, I'll have to get up and close it because I get scared—I'm afraid that somebody will come out of the closet.

ACCOUNTANT, FEMALE, 40

I KNEW A GUY in college who had a lucky condom. He always had two condoms with him. One was his lucky one that he kept in his wallet but never used. The wallet had a permanent ring impression from the condom. He always had another one somewhere else on him. When he went out with that lucky condom, he always ended up using the other one. The guy was convinced that the only way he would end up with a woman would be if he had his lucky condom with him.

RADIO HOST, MALE, 35
HIS COLLEGE FRIEND: PROFESSION UNKNOWN, 36

IF I CAN'T FALL ASLEEP, I'll cover myself with two blankets. It makes me feel warmer, like I'm back in the womb, and then I can fall asleep. In the summer we have the air conditioner on, so it still applies.

JOURNALIST, MALE, 45

MY ARMS MUST BE COVERED when I sleep no matter how warm it is, so I always wear a long-sleeved top to bed. I don't know why, but it feels better when my arms are covered. I usually wear a polo shirt with underwear in the summer and a polo shirt or sweatshirt with pajama bottoms in the winter depending on how cold it is. My skin is sensitive and some materials irritate my skin, especially the skin on my upper body. I can't always find a pajama top that is as soft as my polo shirts. I'm not as particular about my legs.

LAWYER, MALE, 55

I have to vacuum my floor every night before I go to sleep. It has to be clean.

COLLEGE STUDENT, FEMALE, 20

I KEEP A MENTAL LISTING of when I've made love to my wife. During the course of a week if I've noticed that it's going past three times, I'll cut back even if I want more just to make her want more. Absence makes the heart grow fonder but if you go too long it makes the man wander, so you have to be careful with that.

TELEVISION FILM DIRECTOR, MALE, 39

MY FRIEND ADVISED ME to never have sex with my socks on—it's bad luck. So whenever I have sex I always take my socks off.

CIVIL ENGINEER, MALE, 33
HIS FRIEND: UNEMPLOYED, 33

BEFORE I GO TO BED every night, I go around the house doing the usual things, such as turning off all the lights, the TV, and whatever else is on. The very last thing I have to do before I go to bed is to check the front door to make sure it's locked. If I have to get up in the middle of the night to go to the bathroom, or perhaps close some windows because it might have started to rain, or get a glass of milk, I will have to check the door again before I go back to bed even though I know I locked it earlier. (I'm not senile, yet!) No matter what, it has to be the last thing I do before I go to bed.

My place is a simple condo. I've often wondered what I would do if I lived in a house that had several levels and several exterior doors. If I had to go downstairs, would I check the door several times? I'm not sure but deep down inside I suspect the answer would be yes!

RADIO HOST, MALE, 46

I HIDE MY ALARM CLOCK well under my bed so it's tough for me to get to. I'm assured of waking up because in order to turn it off, I have to get up and really stretch to reach it and turn it off.

HIS FRIEND: He's never late.

CONTRACT MANAGER, DEFENSE, MALE, 28

MY HUSBAND always goes to bed without socks, but within an hour he has to put them on no matter what the temperature is. He tries and tries not to wear them but he always ends up putting them on.

DANCE INSTRUCTOR, FEMALE, 35

HER HUSBAND: TECHNICIAN, TELEPHONE COMPANY, 35

I SLEEP WITH THREE BLANKETS all year round but they're not all on top of me. One blanket is on me and the other two are rolled up on each side of me, almost as though a body is next to me. I need to have symmetry. If my girlfriend is sleeping next to me, then I just have one rolled-up blanket on my other side. It's almost like I'm entombed in blankets.

WEB DESIGNER, MALE, 36

I CAN'T GO TO BED unless my room is clean, everything is put away, and there's no mess on the floor. It doesn't matter how late I get home or how tired I am, I have to straighten up or I can't sleep. Messy things anywhere else don't bother me.

STUDENT, JUNIOR, FEMALE, 20

I ALWAYS SLEEP with a pillow over my face. There's one behind me and one on my face. I've always liked pillows on my head and even if I turn sideways, I sleep with it on my head. When I was younger, my mom used to rub my temples, so maybe that's why I like the pressure across my forehead and my eyes.

EDITORIAL ASSISTANT, PUBLISHING, FEMALE, 24

MY WIFE FOLDS THE SHEETS from the foot of the bed going toward the head of the bed about two feet. I fold it the opposite way, about two feet from the head of the bed to the foot of the bed. She thinks the bed looks neater her way because none of the sheet is hanging out from the bottom. Also, when she gets into bed, the sheet already comes right up to her neck. I find it more manageable my way because I can unfold it right from where I am and pull it up toward me. I don't have to get up and go to the bottom of the bed to unfold it. We always argue about that.

JR: Who wins?
Whoever makes the bed.

BUSINESS ANALYST, IT FIRM, MALE, 34
HIS WIFE: HOUSEWIFE, 33

I have to shake my right foot to fall asleep. I was rocked to bed as a child, so it may have stemmed from my childhood. I'm told that when I fall asleep, my foot stops moving. It's really bad on dates. "Hmmmmm, what's wrong with this guy?" they must think.

MEDIA SUPERVISOR, ADVERTISING, MALE, "I DON'T REVEAL MY AGE"

WHEN IT GETS DOWN to seriously sleeping, my partner will barricade himself from me with a row of pillows so that I don't cross over on his section of the bed because I move a lot during the evening. The barricade stays in place and solves the problem.

PRODUCT DESIGNER, MALE, 43
HIS PARTNER: INTERIOR DESIGNER, MALE, 50

WHEN NOBODY IS HOME, I sleep on the couch rather than in my bedroom. I don't really know why but it may be because I've always lived with other people and if I'm sleeping in the living room, I feel as though other people are around and I'm not alone. Or it could be because I'm not allowed to sleep on the couch when other people are around.

ASPIRING ARCHITECT, MALE, 27

YEARS AGO WHEN I WAS IN COLLEGE, my roommate would sneeze three times when he got into bed—every single night. Then he would go to sleep.

JR: Did he sneeze three times other times?
No, just when he got into bed.

JR: Why?
I have no idea and he didn't either.

LAWYER, MALE, 59

HIS FORMER COLLEGE ROOMMATE: PROFESSION UNKNOWN, 59

I SLEEP WITH A LOT OF PILLOWS. If I'm lying on my side I have to have a body pillow between my knees, a pillow under my head, another pillow under my feet. I use a minimum of three pillows, up to six. I have a specific arrangement of pillows for each position. If I'm on my back then there's a couple of pillows under my legs, there's one under my head, the body pillow is holding up either my right or left arm, cushioning that side of me.

PRODUCTION ARTIST, ADVERTISING, MALE, 41

THE LAST WORDS I MUST HEAR before I can turn the TV off to go to sleep is somebody saying something positive. It has to be a positive or uplifting comment or word like "success" or "moving forward." I always want something positive to happen before I leave the room or turn the TV off.

Also, the last thing I look at before I switch the light off is the success poster on my wall. It's one of those motivational-type golf pictures. Some people dream of success while other people wake up and work hard at it.

SALESMAN, POWER COMPANY, MALE, 26

Clothes Encounters of the Strange Kind

No matter where I shop,
Or from whence each bargain hails,
If anybody questions,
I tell them "Bloomingdale's."

MY SOCKS HAVE TO BE SMILING when I put them in the drawer. When you roll up socks and flip one opening over the other, the little shape that's formed at the end of the ball looks like a smile. It's cheerful to open my drawer and see all the socks smiling! I also arrange the socks from lightest on the left to darkest on the right.

VICE PRESIDENT, INSTITUTIONAL TEXTILE SALES, MALE, 43

I WANT THE BELT IN THE PANTS before I put them on. That way I don't miss a loop in the back and when I get the pants on I can immediately secure the pants.

RADIO HOST, MALE, 48

MY WIFE FOLDS HER DIRTY CLOTHES but here's the weird part: She folds them differently than she does the clean ones. That way she can tell the difference. If I'm home and I fold the clothes after taking them out of the dryer, she asks me whether they're clean or dirty because she can't tell. The worst part of the whole thing is that our fifteen-year-old daughter has started doing the same thing.

PHYSICAL THERAPIST, MALE, 46
HIS WIFE: MEDICAL PROFESSIONAL, 43

WHEN I HAVE TO DRY an article of clothing in a hurry, I'll put it into the microwave and heat it up.

JR: Great idea! What setting do you recommend?
It depends on how damp it is. You have to use your judgment.

RETIRED, FEMALE, 78

MY CLOTHING IS SELECTED based on the color of the shoes that I'm wearing that day. I alternate the color of my shoes every day. I have black and brown shoes. Monday, Wednesday, and Friday are typically black shoe days. Tuesday and Thursday are brown shoe days. Dark clothing—gray slacks, navy blue— goes with the black shoes. Khakis and more relaxed, casual clothing are worn with brown shoes. Essentially it started as soon as I started working in my professional career, because when I get up in the morning I have to get dressed quickly to catch the train to work. This is an easy way to alternate clothes and keep on schedule.

JR: Has anyone noticed your system?
No.

COMMUNICATIONS CONSULTANT, MALE, 50

FREQUENTLY, I FORGET that I wore the shirt I'm wearing today, yesterday, and maybe even the day before that. People often ask me, "Do you wear the same shirt every day?" So I lie and say, "No, I have three of the same shirts."

PHOTOGRAPHER, MALE, 62

EXPIRATION IS AN EVENT that happens once a month on the third Friday. It's an event where certain contracts or options expire. Four times a year, in March, June, September, and December, there is a major expiration event called triple witching when the contracts for stock index futures, stock index options, and stock options all expire on the same day. The simultaneous expirations often result in a huge volume of trades. There is a tremendous amount of money at stake. Our calculations have to be dead-on accurate because all our P&L for the month is going to be based on this. What we generally do is stay late and just go over figures to make sure everything is accurate.

Some of us even go to a hotel room just to make sure that nothing can possibly go wrong in the morning. In the morning, we don't shave, we all wear the ugliest tie we can find, and we're on our honor not to change our underwear. (When I studied in college, I didn't shave because possibly some molecule of information was stuck in a whisker and, God forbid, I should shave it off.) I have no idea why but that's what we do. Sometimes people will see me in the bathroom and they'll look at me and say, "Oh, it must be expiration," and it better be an expiration because otherwise they're commenting on my clothes or my hygiene.

CHIEF INFORMATION OFFICER, TECHNOLOGIST FOR TRADING FIRM, MALE, 38

PEOPLE THINK I'M CRAZY because I have my pockets tailored. They're always too deep and if you put too much in them, they hang down the side of your legs and bang against them. I cut them off and make them shorter.

BRANCH MANAGER, BANK, MALE, 40s

I DON'T CARE how tired I am, if I kick my shoes off without untieing the laces, I always have to get up, untie them, arrange them neatly and put the loose laces inside the shoes. And I don't want them to be pigeon-toed, one way or the other way. They've got to be very neat, like they're on a rack.

CIVIL SERVANT, UNITED NATIONS, MALE, 31

MY FRIEND WRITES DOWN everything he wears on his calendar so he doesn't wear it again for three weeks or longer if possible. I've observed him and paid attention to when I saw an outfit repeated and it was exactly three weeks.

COLLEGE JUNIOR, MALE, 22
HIS FRIEND: COLLEGE JUNIOR, 22

IN COLLEGE I'd bring exactly half the number of pairs of underwear I would need to last me until the time I'd be going home with the notion that underwear is reversible. My mother did my laundry and I didn't have to carry too much on the plane. It ranged from fifteen to thirty pair for thirty to sixty days. Now I'm married and my wife would leave me if I were to reverse my underwear at the age of thirty-four.

BOND PORTFOLIO MANAGER, MALE, 34

I PLAY POKER every Thursday night and I wear a different baseball cap to the game each week. I wear the New York Giants football cap, the San Francisco Giants baseball cap, or the Boston Celtics basketball cap. Whichever one of those teams is doing the best, that's the cap I'll wear. If things aren't going well in the card game, I'll turn the cap around backward, or put it on at a different angle.

JOURNALIST, MALE, 41

I WILL ONLY ALLOW my clothes to be hung up on white plastic hangers. No exceptions. It drives me crazy if the hangers are any other color.

AUTOMOTIVE MECHANIC, MALE, 28

THE COLORS OF MY HANGERS have to match the colors of my clothing. I hang a blue skirt or pants on a blue hanger. A red dress is hung on a red hanger. My white shirts are on white hangers and so on.

STUDENT, FEMALE, 21

I ONCE UNINTENTIONALLY wore one black shoe and one brown shoe to an important meeting. Thankfully, no one noticed. The meeting was a huge success. Now, whenever there is an important occasion or event, I will deliberately wear one black shoe and one brown shoe hoping it will continue to have a positive outcome.

EXECUTIVE, PHARMACEUTICALS, MALE, 58

I HANG ALL THE SHORT-SLEEVED SHIRTS and pants so the hooks of the hangers are facing toward the rear of the closet, but I hang all the long-sleeved shirts with the hooks of the hangers facing the front. I do this for neatness and organization.

POLICE OFFICER, MALE, 36

MY FIANCÉ DATES and numbers his pants. For example, he will write "'05, pants #3" on the label inside the pants. When I first started seeing him, I thought that was so strange.

 JR: When he throws a pair of pants out, does he retire that number?

He still has pants going back five or six years because he doesn't gain any weight.

RADIO CALLER, FEMALE, PROFESSION AND AGE UNKNOWN

I GET DRESSED CLOCKWISE. Wherever I am in the room, I just head in a clockwise direction to the next item or article of clothing and put that on. First I see my watch, then comes my underwear drawer, socks are next, shirt, tie, and slacks after that, finally my sport jacket. And if I don't do that, inevitably, I forget to put something on, like my belt.

RADIO SPORTS BROADCASTER, MALE, 29

I SUCKED MY THUMB until I was about twelve years old. While I sucked my thumb I held a piece of soft fabric that was from a pair of pajamas I had. I'm thirty-one years old now and I still have that piece of fabric. I will tuck that piece of fabric in my pocket for good luck or comfort if I go on an interview or for some other important event, even though I know in my mind that it's nuts.

NEW MEDIA MANAGER, INTERNET COMPANY, MALE, 31

THE MINUTE I WALK IN THE DOOR I begin peeling all my clothing off until I'm naked. I don't wear any clothes in my apartment unless I have a guest over. I make my phone calls in the nude, I eat in the nude, and I sleep in the nude. When I'm by myself I prefer to be nude.

JR: Aren't you cold in the winter?

No, and I keep the windows open all year round—I like it cold. Sometimes if it's very cold, I'll be nude and have a wool cap on.

CARPENTER, MALE, 27

I iron all of my husband's clothing in the order that he gets dressed. I iron his undershirts first because that's what goes on him first. Then I iron his regular T-shirt, then his dress shirt, then his shorts or pants.

SECRETARY, DEVELOPMENT COMPANY, FEMALE, 26

MY MOTHER'S IDEA of a fashion statement is to wear everything in the same color. If she wears green, she'll put on green pants, a green sweatshirt, green socks, and green shoes—they're never the same shade. One Christmas, she thought it would be nice to wear red, so she wore a red dress, red necklace, red nylons, and red shoes. My mother and father got into a fight about her attire and wanted my opinion. I, of course, didn't want to get involved. She said, "Dad thinks that I have too much red on, what do you think?" "No, Mom, I really don't want to give you an opinion—you just have to be comfortable wearing what you're wearing." But she talked me into it so I said, "Okay, Mom, you look like one big red tomato." She exchanged only the nylons for a neutral shade. She got indignant, stormed off, and said, "Well, I'm going to wear this anyway!"

MANAGER, AEROSPACE ENGINEERING, FEMALE, 39

HER MOTHER: RETIRED SECRETARY, 62

WHEN TRAVELING, I pack enough underwear to last more than the length of my stay, but I have to wash them as soon as I can as I wear them. I'm out of town and the outfit that I wore yesterday is already washed and hanging in the bathroom.

BALLET TEACHER, FEMALE, "SENIOR"

I HAVE TWO PILES of clothing in my room—one's clean and one's dirty. The way you tell which pile to put an article of clothing on is to sniff it. If it smells a little rancid it goes on the dirty pile and then I take something off the clean pile to wear that day. You definitely hope you don't grab the clothes off the wrong pile when you're in a hurry or late for work.

PHARMACEUTICAL REPRESENTATIVE, MALE, 30

I HAVE TWO TYPES OF WIRE HANGERS in my closet: metal ones and white ones. If I've worn a shirt more than once, I'll put it on the white hanger so I'll know that after I wear it one more time, it goes into the laundry. In the summer I'll wear a shirt twice and in the winter maybe three times. This enables me to differentiate those shirts that have been worn more than once by the color of the hanger. My pants go on wooden hangers and there's no specific number of wearings for a pair of pants.

WORD PROCESSOR, MALE, 64

WHEN I STARTED to take flying lessons, I happened to be wearing black panties and the flying lessons went well. To this day I make sure that I wear black panties when I go flying (new ones, of course, not the original pair). It's for good luck.

COMPUTER SPECIALIST, FOREIGN MISSION, FEMALE, 47

MY BROTHER WEARS two pairs of socks because he feels that his ankles are too thin and it bulks up his ankles a bit. He's been doing this since he was about fourteen years old. He started working out at fourteen and his whole body grew except his ankles. He buys his shoes a half size larger as a result.

STOCKBROKER, MALE, 27
HIS BROTHER: STORE OWNER, 25

I MATCH THE COLOR of the perfume or lotion that I use to the color of the clothes that I'm wearing. If I'm wearing red clothing, I'll wear strawberry or apple perfume. If I'm wearing green, I'll wear the pear or watermelon because watermelon is green outside. If I'm wearing black, I'll usually wear a clear perfume like Calvin Klein Obsession or Eternity because they're more mature scents. I have a total of about forty or fifty lotions and perfumes.

CLIENT SERVICES, PUBLIC RELATIONS, FEMALE, 24

AFTER MANY YEARS OF SHOPPING, I decided that it would be much easier to locate clothing in my closet if I organized them according to color, not according to style. I really freak out if I find something in the wrong color group. The crazy part is I have absolutely no idea how it started, but now I'm maniacal about it.

TEXTILE DESIGNER, FEMALE, 57

IN THE CLOSET are five pairs of sneakers that must be lined up from worst on the left to best on the right—gardening sneakers, workout sneakers, play sneakers, running around sneakers, and dress sneakers. When the worst sneakers get so bad that they can't be worn, they get thrown away and the rest get moved down one place and a brand new pair of sneakers goes into the best position.

Same with jeans. I have five pairs of jeans also lined up from worst on the left to best on the right. If I buy a new pair of jeans, it gets the best position on the right, the others move down one, and the crummiest one on the left gets thrown away.

PAROLE OFFICER, MALE, 53

AFTER I'VE GONE TO THE BATHROOM, I have to pull up my underwear and whatever else I'm wearing at the same time because I don't like the feeling of just underwear. I have to have something over them or else it feels disgusting.

STUDENT, FEMALE, 9

WHENEVER I REMOVE my underwear, even if I put a clean pair on a minute earlier, I must put a fresh pair of underwear on. If I'm going swimming, for example, when I return I will not put on the same pair of underwear that I had on before I went swimming even if they are clean. The one I was wearing no longer feels fresh. I know it's totally irrational, but that's how it is, so I have to have a lot of underwear!

REHABILITATION COUNSELOR, FEMALE, 55

My sister wears all her T-shirts an equal number of times so none of them will get offended.

MUSICIAN, FEMALE, 25

HER SISTER: STUDENT, 16

MY COWORKER Todd never unties his necktie. He loosens it and slips it off over his head. When he wants to wear it again, he slips it back on over his head. He wears the same tie every other day—I think he only has two ties. He admitted that he's lazy and can't be bothered with tying or untying his tie.

ENGINEER, MALE, 36

HIS COWORKER: ENGINEER, 36

I DELIBERATELY PUT A LITTLE HOLE in one of the socks in each pair I own to discourage anyone from borrowing them. Members of my family used to steal my socks. Later my roommates tried to borrow them. If it has a hole in it they no longer want it.

JR to Reader: He showed me the hole.

SALES ENGINEER, INTERNET COMPANY, MALE, 32

I ONLY BUY DESIGNER CLOTHES. And I always pay full price. Never would I buy discount clothing or buy something on sale. It's just a bad habit I have.

COLLEGE STUDENT, FEMALE, 20

I IRON MY SHIRTS when they come back from the dry cleaners because I don't like the little impressions formed on the sleeves from the hangers. Each month I use three cans of heavy spray starch. I actually go through about thirty-six cans a year. I even spray starch underwear and socks. I iron the entire household's clothing. My wife hasn't turned on the iron since we got married. I keep an iron in my office so I can re-press my shirt if I go out at night.

JR to Reader: His shirt was the crispest, whitest shirt I've ever seen!

DIRECTOR, TRADE MARKETING, COSMETICS COMPANY, MALE, 34

I GET RID OF ALL MY SOCKS and underwear at the same time about every three years. Then I go out and get all new ones. When they're all new, they all last the same amount of time. I rotate them after I wash them. I put the freshly cleaned ones in the back of the drawer and slide the others forward so they all get used the same amount.

INTERIOR DESIGNER, MALE, 46

WHEN I WAS YOUNG, I could never find a raincoat that fit me properly. I finally found one when I was a student. I still have it and I wear it as many times as I can. In fact, it's in my office right now. I love Humphrey Bogart and the movie *Casablanca* and when I'm wearing that raincoat and find myself in an airport or train station, even though I'm not a smoker, I pretend I'm smoking a cigarette. In my raincoat, I feel like I'm Humphrey Bogart and I go through the motions of smoking and I just love the feeling. I have the urge to mimic him every single time I wear the raincoat. I've never told this story to anybody—my wife doesn't even know this story!

PARK MANAGER, MALE, 26

I TRY TO MAINTAIN A MINIMUM amount of clothes in my clothing inventory. I do not replace an article of clothing until it is worn out. My wife sometimes fools me by going out and buying something for me, which messes up my inventory. Protesting doesn't do much good.

RETIRED PHARMACIST, MALE, 75

I HAVE A FRIEND who loves to wear all these handkerchiefs. On any given day he probably wears five handkerchiefs at the same time. One he ties around his neck, one he ties very tight around his forehead—I always tell him to loosen it up so he doesn't cut off the blood circulation to his head. The one around his forehead is tight because it holds down one or two other handkerchiefs that go over his head to protect his bald spots, soak up the sweat, whatever. As a result, he has all these hankies that he has to wash at night after a big day at the beach. Handkerchiefs are always hanging everywhere in our hotel rooms.

ATTORNEY, MALE, 45
HIS FRIEND: SOFTWARE PROGRAMMER, MALE, EARLY 40s

IF I GET CALLED BACK when I go to audition, I wear the same outfit to the callback and if I don't get cast, I never wear those clothes again to an audition.

STUDENT AND ACTRESS, FEMALE, 21

AT THE END OF EACH DAY, my neighbor takes his business shirt off, removes the collar stays, and puts the collar stays in a small manila envelope the size of a business card. He then labels the envelope with a description of the shirt that he took the stays out of.

This same neighbor line dries his socks and underwear even in the wintertime. I've asked him why he does it. He thinks they just smell better that way.

VICE PRESIDENT, INSTITUTIONAL TEXTILE SALES, MALE, 43

HIS NEIGHBOR: LAWYER, 37

All of my favorite clothes must be hung on yellow metal hangers. I acquired the hangers somewhere in the course of my life, I have no idea where, but I have about twenty yellow metal hangers. If a shirt comes out of the laundry and it's one of my favorite shirts, I have to hang it on a yellow metal hanger. This way it's easier to pick out the shirt.

ENGINEER, MALE, 32

MY EX-GIRLFRIEND would not let me get into bed without socks. She hated the feeling of my feet against her legs. She didn't have to wear socks—it was more important that I wore socks.

ASSISTANT MEDIA PLANNER, ADVERTISING, MALE, 24
HIS EX-GIRLFRIEND: ASSISTANT MEDIA PLANNER, ADVERTISING, 23

I IRON MY UNDERWEAR to get the wrinkles out so it's nice and smooth. Wrinkles bother me. In the wintertime when I wear an undershirt, I iron that too. When I'm going out, I also iron my socks so they're nice and fresh and clean. But I only iron the socks on special occasions.

MAINTENANCE MAN, RAILROAD, MALE, 42

WHEN MOST PEOPLE tie their shoelaces, they prop up the foot with the shoe that needs tying. I prop up the foot with the shoe that doesn't need tying and tie the one that's still on the ground.

FINANCIAL PLANNER, MALE, 23

I'VE WORN GLASSES for thirteen years. When I wake up and haven't as yet put on my glasses or at other times when I am briefly not wearing them for some reason, I still find myself trying to push them up the bridge of my nose with my index finger or adjusting them by the temples.

ACCOUNTANT, MALE, 23

MY COWORKER'S THEORY on buying shoes is that she can only buy shoes in even numbers, so she can never buy just one pair of shoes. The minimum number of shoes that she will buy is two. If she sees a pair of shoes that she likes she will have to buy a second pair. If she wants three pairs, she will have to choose a fourth. They don't have to be the same style. To her it's good luck if you buy in even numbers and bad luck if you buy in odd numbers.

FINANCE ANALYST, FEMALE, 31

HER COWORKER: SYSTEMS ANALYST, 40s

I LIKE TO MATCH the color of my underwear to the color of my shirt. I only wear white socks—those don't have to match.

ELECTRICIAN, MALE, 35

I LEAVE DRAWERS, closet doors, and cabinet doors open—it drives my wife crazy! I know there's somebody else around who will shut them after me. We moved and now the lights go on automatically in the closet. My wife mistakenly thought that now I would be cured of leaving the closet door open, but I still leave it open because I always think that I'm going to go back to get something else out.

ATTORNEY, MALE, 55

MY MOTHER BUYS SHOES two sizes larger than her foot because "my size is too tight." Go figure.

LEGAL SECRETARY, FEMALE, 44

HER MOTHER: HOUSEWIFE, 70

I ONLY WEAR TIES with animal motifs. I'm from South Africa, so it makes me feel at home. I have one for each day of the workweek. Monday is elephant day, Tuesday is the big five—the rhino, the elephant, the leopard, the lion, and the buffalo,

Wednesday is the zebra, Thursday is a black-and-white lion, and the elephant again on Friday. It distinguishes me.

COMPUTER CONSULTANT, MALE, 33

I WASH MY CLOTHING whether I've worn them or not. Even clean clothes get washed every week. When clothes are lying around for more than a week I get sensitive to the mustiness because I have hypersensitive smell. I do several loads of laundry a week. That may sound very peculiar to the average person, but I associate it with comfort, so it becomes worth the effort.

DIRECTOR, PUBLIC FOUNDATION AND INVESTOR, MALE, 53

IT'S A KNOWN FACT that most socks, but especially brand new terry cloth socks, can be worn for close to two weeks without washing them. The very thin dress socks are the only exception.

RADIO BROADCASTER, MALE, AGE UNKNOWN

I COLOR COORDINATE MY UNDERWEAR with the outfit that I'm wearing. I'll wear pink if I'm wearing something in the pink family or white if I'm wearing a white outfit. If I don't find a color to match, I'll feel miserable for the whole day. This is a fairly new quirk of mine—I've been doing it for the past couple of years. My husband doesn't even know about it.

TEXTILE DESIGNER, FEMALE, 57

THERE ARE THREE CATEGORIES of shirts in my drawers. The shirts that I like the most make me feel and look the best, so I put those shirts on top in the drawer. The ones in the middle are a little older. The ones toward the bottom have a small stain and I don't necessarily want to wear them. When I get down to the ones I like least, I know that it's time to do my laundry.

COLLEGE STUDENT, FEMALE, 21

I'VE NEVER WORN sandals or thongs—not even for a second, in my life, and I'm forty-seven years old. I have long toes and I think that feet are pretty ugly and I can't imagine why anybody would want their feet to be exposed. When I see people in sandals I think to myself, "How can they wear those sandals? They're so ugly. They must be out of their mind." I don't get it. Wear sneakers if you want to be casual. Some women paint their toenails and it looks disgusting. Women with pumps look terrific. My son thinks it's a riot—he wears sandals constantly.

REDEVELOPMENT EXECUTIVE, MALE, 47

I ALWAYS PUT MY LEFT SHOE on first. If by some chance I'm not thinking and I start putting my right shoe on, I will immediately remove it and put on the left shoe instead.

RETIRED PHARMACIST, MALE, 75

I IRON ON MY FLOOR. It began because I was too lazy to get the ironing board out, but now I actually prefer ironing on the floor. One advantage is that I save some time in the morning because I don't have to take the ironing board out. I just put a towel down on the floor, bend down, and iron on the towel. There's always a towel on the floor when I leave and people wonder why.

SALES ASSISTANT, INSTITUTIONAL SALES, FEMALE, 23

SOMETIMES WHEN I NEGLECT to cut my toenails, the nails on my big toes make a hole in my socks. When that happens, I switch the socks to the opposite feet. The one on my left foot goes on my right foot and vice versa. The holes then line up with my small toes and I make new holes. This way the socks last longer. It annoys me that my toe made a hole in a sock that is otherwise in good condition. With this technique I get a little more "mileage" out of them.

ATTORNEY, MALE, 55

WHEN I TRY ON A PAIR OF PANTS or a shirt in the store and I like the way it fits, I go back to get another one because that one's been tried on and I want one that is brand new.

COLLEGE STUDENT, FEMALE, 21

I wear a bathing suit under my clothes instead of undergarments because it's all one piece and it's easy. I don't have to worry about the waist binding or finding a bra and underpants—it's all together. I just push the crotch aside when I go to the bathroom.

OFFICE MANAGER, FEMALE, 50

I FREQUENTLY DON'T HAVE very much time and I'm too lazy to iron my shirts or my pants, so I just hang them all up in the bathroom and turn on the shower for forty-five minutes to an hour. It's probably doing wonders to the linoleum and paint in my bathroom! Right now, in fact, I have six shirts and two pants hanging up on the rod—my wardrobe for this week.

FINANCIAL WRITER, MALE, 29

I KEEP A PAIR OF SOCKS in my drawer at work. They are not for my feet. They're for my hands. When I feel cold, I put the socks on my hands to warm up a bit. I don't always have gloves available. My colleagues often ridicule me about this.

LAWYER, MALE, 53

MY CLOTHES HAVE TO BE IN A GIG LINE like in the military. I was in the military, but I've been doing this since I was four years old. The seam of my shirt has to align with my belt buckle, which has to be aligned with the zipper flap of my pants. It must be a perfect line going from my neck all the way down to the bottom of my zipper.

ACTOR, MALE, 27

WHEN I GO TO THE GYM and I change from my work clothes into my workout clothes, I take my right sock and stick it inside my left sock. After I shower and I get back into my work clothes, I know which sock goes on which foot. My big toes go where they fit and I don't have a bulging area on the outside of my sock since they are on the correct feet.

STRUCTURAL ENGINEER, MALE, 48

I KEEP MY SHOES on top of each other instead of side by side to save space in the closet. What's odd is that I put the shoes that I've walked around in during the day at the bottom of the pile, which requires me to dismantle and rebuild the stack. This enables my shoes to be worn in a logical progression. To prevent them from toppling over, I start the bottom pair away from the wall and lean the stack toward the back wall.

TECHNICAL CONSULTANT, INTERNET COMPANY, MALE, 26

I VARY THE DIRECTION that I feed my belts into the belt loops of my pants to maintain the health and "good-looking beltness" appearance of my belts. I evaluate the condition of the belts hanging on the belt rack and I decide, "Today we need to start the reconditioning of this belt." I then start feeding it in the opposite direction for a few days. I will usually feed to the left until I notice that the belt is developing a kink, and then I will start feeding to the right. It's a very awkward sensation but I force myself to do it.

ARCHITECT, MALE, 32

I don't wear any underwear in the winter. I like the cold breeze. In the summer I do wear underwear because if I start to sweat, the pants kind of grab and get a little clingy.

ACCOUNT EXECUTIVE, MALE, 32

THE NECK OF MY SHIRT has to be pulled over my face up to my mouth when I watch TV. I can't watch TV without doing it. It is the only time that I do it. I have no recollection of when or why it began. I usually don't notice that I am doing it until someone points it out. I think it's like a security blanket (although I never had one of those) because the more into a show/movie I am, the more likely I am to do it. I don't do it in public.

BROADCAST TRAFFIC COORDINATOR, FEMALE, 28

WHEN I WASH MY CLOTHES I always put the freshly washed items at the back of the drawer and take items to wear from the front, continuing in order. That ensures an even wear for all my undergarments, socks, and casual shirts.

ARCHITECT, MALE, 60

JEANS ARE ALL CUT slightly differently when they're manufactured and each pair will fit your body slightly differently. Whenever I buy a pair of jeans, I'll try on every pair in the shop in my size and ask the stockperson to get every pair in my size from the back so I can find a pair that fits me perfectly.

WEB SITE PRODUCER, MALE, 28

I must have a new pair of running shoes in my closet. I won't wear my new pair without having another new pair to replace them.

DIRECTOR OF STORE COMMUNICATIONS AND TRAINING, MALE, 32

I KEEP THREE PURSES with almost identical items in each purse. I just remove my wallet when I'm ready to go out and put it in the purse I take with me. It's a pain to have to switch from purse to purse, so I'm prepared with three that are always ready to go. All three contain tissues, lip gloss, mirror, comb, et cetera, everything except my wallet and a book if I'm reading one. I have a black purse, a tan one, and a red one.

COLLEGE STUDENT, FEMALE, 25

IF I ACCIDENTALLY put on my underwear or any piece of clothing inside out or backward while getting dressed, I will have to wear it that way all day or remove it, spit on it, and then put it back on. It's bad luck to put it back on without spitting on it. When I fold my clean underwear, I try to fold it the right way and put it in the drawer the right way to avoid accidentally putting it on backward. You can imagine how uncomfortable it is wearing underwear backward because things don't line up where they should.

RELATIONSHIP MANAGER, ADVERTISING SOFTWARE, MALE, 41

AFTER WEARING MY SHOES and socks all day, I find that I have sock fuzz between my toes when I take my socks off. So I take my socks and floss between my toes to get it all out. Some socks are less fuzzy than other socks, so I don't have to floss as much.

PROJECT MANAGER, TECHNOLOGY, MALE, 36

The Howard Hughes Syndrome

Doorknobs and faucets
Are useful you see,
But I hope that their germs
Never rub off on me.

I IRON THE NEWSPAPER before I will read it. The *New York Times* is delivered to my doorstep every morning. Before I read it, I iron the outside of each section. All my things are ironed or wiped with 70 percent alcohol to sterilize them. I have been doing this for years to protect myself from germs.

ARTIST/SCULPTOR, FEMALE, AGE NOT DISCLOSED

MY HUSBAND IS MR. QUIRKAROONIE. When we go to a restaurant, he won't allow the silverware to touch anything but the plate. If the silverware is wrapped up in a napkin, he won't unwrap it until the plate is in front of him. Then he unwraps the napkin and puts the silverware on the plate. If the silverware is set on the napkin but there is no bread plate to put them on, he won't put the napkin on his lap until his food arrives because he wouldn't have anywhere to set the silverware. The silverware absolutely cannot touch the table, the tablecloth, or anything except the plate.

PUBLICIST, FEMALE, 36
HER HUSBAND: HUMAN RESOURCES MANAGER, 38

I CARRY A LARGE plastic shopping bag with me. When I go to the hairdresser or somewhere where I have to remove my coat and hang it up, I put it into the shopping bag and hang the shopping bag up so my coat doesn't touch someone else's coat and get contaminated.

RETIRED TEACHER, FEMALE, 74

AT A FAST-FOOD RESTAURANT I never take the top lid to cover my soda. It may have fallen on the floor and someone may have picked it up and put it back. I'll take one from the middle of the stack. And when I buy coffee to go, I don't like when the counterperson puts the lid on, because their hands touched it. If there were a choice, I'd prefer to put the lid on myself. I always remove that lid and throw it away and then get my own lid from deep inside the lid rack.

ACCOUNT MANAGER, RETAIL, FEMALE, 54

WHEN I GO THROUGH A REVOLVING DOOR, I'm ecstatic when one person is in front of me and another person is behind me because then I don't have to touch the door to push it since they are both pushing it. Or if someone goes through a revolving door before me and gives it an energetic push then I can run in and get through without touching it while it's still spinning.

REAL ESTATE BROKER, FEMALE, 53

I NEVER USE A HAND BLOWER, because people don't fully dry their hands, so germs harvest inside the nozzle and start to grow. When the blower is activated, it's actually blowing bacteria all over your hands as it's drying them.

EDITOR, TV NEWS, FEMALE, 22

I BRING SEVERAL TOWELS with me on vacation. I use one to put over the pillow because I don't want my face to be in contact with pillowcases other than my own. And I use another one for showering because I don't want to use theirs.

ADMINISTRATIVE ASSISTANT, FEMALE, 41

MY UNCLE will not eat anybody else's food. He doesn't go to restaurants and if a friend or relative invites him over, he will go but he won't eat the food. He'll politely decline and say that he already ate. He'll refrain from eating food that he hasn't prepared. He won't even eat his sister's (my mother's) food.

Occasionally, if my mother is at his house and he actually sees her preparing the food and it meets his standards, then he may eat it.

BOND PORTFOLIO MANAGER, MALE, 35

HIS UNCLE: RETIRED EDUCATOR, 61

I CALL IT "Clean Hand, Dirty Hand." I operate the mouse with my right hand and I eat with my left hand. I try to keep one hand clean for eating. Who knows who's handled the mouse before me? The only hand that touches food is my left hand. I also wash my hands frequently.

IMAGING FOR MAGAZINE, MALE, 30

I HAVE A FRIEND who doesn't like anybody to touch her napkins or towels, ever. At a wedding, she won't ever get up because she doesn't want the wait staff to fold her napkin and put it back on the table. If someone touches it she won't use it again.

GRANTS ADMINISTRATOR FOR A FOUNDATION, FEMALE, 38

HER FRIEND: GRANTS ADMINISTRATOR FOR A FOUNDATION, 35

I'VE HEARD THAT PEOPLE in dirty environments like prison open a box of cigarettes from the bottom so that the fingers touch the tobacco end of the cigarette when it is removed. The filter end, which is put in the mouth, stays clean.

GRAPHIC DESIGNER, MALE, 32

ABOUT ONCE A MONTH, I put my toothbrushes in the dishwasher and run them through the cycle. The water is very hot and it sterilizes them.

PRODUCTION ASSISTANT, TELEVISION STUDIO, FEMALE, 48

AT THE GYM, I wash my hands every ten or fifteen minutes and try not to touch my face because the bars on exercise machines have filthy germs. People sneeze, cough, or wipe off their sweat and then touch the bars. The next person—who could be me—gets all the germs from the previous person by touching the bars or by handling the equipment.

ACCOUNTANT, MALE, 25

AFTER GROCERY SHOPPING, I do not enter my apartment with the bags or cartons of groceries. I unpack them in the hallway by bringing each item into my apartment individually. I don't want to risk bringing any roaches into my home.

ADVERTISING DIRECTOR, INTERNET SALES, FEMALE, 43

I'VE BEEN LAUNDERING MONEY for years. I put a little bit of Lysol liquid cleaner in some water. It forms nice little suds when I splash the money around. Then I rinse the money and lay them down flat. They dry beautifully—like they just came out of the mint.

JR to Reader: I tried it and it works!

RADIO CALLER, FEMALE, PROFESSION AND AGE UNKNOWN

IT'S DISGUSTING TO SIT DOWN on a seat immediately after it was occupied by someone else. It's usually warm from the previous person's body heat. I don't know that person and even if I did, it's still gross. Who knows, they may have passed gas. If possible, I'll wait for it to cool off or neutralize from air circulation. If it's a seat on a crowded bus or train, I'll try to "reserve" it by putting a package or a shopping bag or my briefcase on it for a few minutes before I sit down. This is not always possible because it's hard to endure the resentful glares of other passengers who would like to sit down but can't because an available seat is being occupied by a tote bag.

FINANCIAL ANALYST, FEMALE, 47

WHEN I REMOVE A STRAW from the straw dispenser, I discard the first straw and go for the second or third straw because surely that first straw is contaminated. The second one must be cleaner.

HAIR STYLIST, MALE, 36

IT NEVER FAILS to astound me when a waiter serves a drink by holding the glass at the top with their fingers surrounding the rim. How unsanitary and insensitive that is! Who wants to drink through someone else's fingerprints and germs? Don't restaurants train their wait staff not to do that?

OWNER, REAL ESTATE COMPANY, MALE, 49

MY FRIEND WILL NOT ALLOW PEOPLE to touch the sheets that she sleeps in. She knows people will sit on her bed if she has a party so she covers her bedspread with a duvet cover. When everyone leaves she takes the duvet cover off of her bedspread and changes the sheets underneath just in case someone accidentally touched them.

SUPERVISOR, MEDIA COMPANY RESEARCH DEPARTMENT, FEMALE, 26

HER FRIEND: INTERIOR DESIGNER, FEMALE, 26

> I wash the dish rack before I wash the dishes. I don't want to put clean dishes on a dish rack that is not immaculately clean.

SALES PLANNER, ADVERTISING, FEMALE, 23

IN THE MORNING I get dressed and apply my makeup, including lipstick. When I get to work I always pour myself a cup of coffee. I hold the mug with the handle in my left hand, so that all the lipstick comes off on that side of the mug. Then I turn the mug around, holding it with my right hand and drink from the clean side. I'm squeamish about drinking through lipstick, even my own.

TEACHER, FEMALE, 60

I'VE BEEN THINKING of confronting the Mobil people about this. I pick up my coffee on the way to work at a Mobil on-the-run gas convenience stop. They have a very nice coffee section but the stir sticks are horizontal. That means that somebody else may have handled the stir stick that I put in my coffee. If they would position them vertically, I wouldn't freak out about it because I don't care if someone touches the top as long as they don't touch the part that I'm sticking into my coffee. They should do something about that.

RADIO HOST, MALE, 57

I NEVER EAT MINTS from the bowl near the cash register in a restaurant if they are unwrapped and exposed. There are statistics in surveys that have been conducted about the number of people who don't wash their hands after using the rest room. It's quite a large percentage. That has sworn me off mints forever.

VICE PRESIDENT, HUMAN RESOURCES, PUBLIC RELATIONS FIRM, MALE, 43

IN PUBLIC REST ROOMS, I throw away the first four feet of toilet paper in case it touched the floor and got rolled back up. If possible, I'll turn the toilet paper roll to the *correct* position of down the back.

POLICY ANALYST/WRITER FOR COUNTY GOVERNMENT, FEMALE, 44

IF SOMEONE BEGINS SWEEPING while I am eating, it bothers me so much that I have to grab my food and leave. There are always dust particles flying everywhere and I don't want dust or pieces of lint or—even worse—hair, landing on my food or in my drink. People take a bite out of their hamburger knowing that there's lint on it. I just can't deal with it.

JR: Will you eat outdoors?

I like eating outdoors because then the lint is constantly moving. It just floats away in the open space.

MEDIA SUPERVISOR, ADVERTISING, MALE, "I DON'T REVEAL MY AGE"

MY FRIEND would rather not wash his hands than use soap that someone else has used. When he visits someone, the host has to search around the house for a new bar of soap.

FINANCIAL PLANNER, FEMALE, 24

HER FRIEND: PAINTER (ARTIST), 24

MY HUSBAND KICKS the toilet seat up with his foot because he doesn't want to touch it, even in our own home. I would frequently hear these loud clanks in the bathroom and I would think, "What the heck is he doing?" One time I peeked in and I saw him kicking up the seat, and when I asked him about it, he explained that he didn't want to touch the toilet seat. He's very germ conscious. There is a mark on the lid from all the banging.

MERCHANDISE PLANNER, FEMALE, 47
HER HUSBAND: ENGINEER, 47

ROOM SERVICE IN A HOTEL is one luxury that I have no interest in because eating in a hotel room is a turnoff to me. There's something unappetizing about eating in a room where so many people have lived and slept. Most hotel rooms are stuffy and have a chemical odor from years of spraying disinfectant or deodorizing sprays. I just can't do it.

ART DIRECTOR, FEMALE, 51

MY MOTHER-IN-LAW was a nurse for over forty years, so she's germ paranoid. When she goes grocery shopping at the supermarket, she washes virtually everything with soap and water before it goes in the refrigerator. If you look at the bottom of containers in the store, some of them are actually pretty dirty.

INVESTMENT MANAGEMENT, BANK, MALE, 37
HIS MOTHER-IN-LAW: RETIRED NURSE, 72

After I shake someone's hand, I go to the bathroom to wash my hands or use a wet-wipe because their hand may have germs.

ACCOUNT EXECUTIVE, FEMALE, 32

MY FRIEND EATS EVERYTHING with a knife and fork, including sandwiches, because he doesn't want to touch any food with his hands. He's never picked up a sandwich with his hands. When he has a meatball sub, he cuts it up. He eats buffalo chicken wings—which everybody in the world picks up with their hands—with a knife and fork. I've asked him why he doesn't just wash his hands. He's never given me a satisfactory answer. He just says, "I'm not going to pick it up with my hands—that's all there is to it."

MANAGING DIRECTOR, INVESTMENT MANAGEMENT, MALE, 40
HIS FRIEND: VICE PRESIDENT, INVESTMENT MANAGEMENT FIRM, 26

I CAN'T EAT NEAR A BATHROOM in a restaurant or in somebody's house. Also, if the bathroom door is open, I can't eat. If I'm seated near a bathroom, I ask to be moved as far away as possible.

VIDEO EDITOR, FEMALE, 28

WHEN I TRAVEL, I carry my toothbrush in one of those two-piece tube containers. I put my toothbrush in "bristles last" because that way they're the farthest from the little drain holes. Ya gotta assume that if stuff can get out, stuff can get in. And if I'm camping instead of hoteling, then I'll even stuff a cotton ball down there as a germ block for good measure. Even though I'm a regular hand-washer, there's still something dirtier about the handle end. Yeah, I know my mouth is full of germs, too, so don't bother telling me I'm ridiculous. Wait a minute—I forgot who I'm talking to. Only you would understand how much thought went into making the decision of "bristles last versus bristles first."

POLICY ANALYST/WRITER FOR COUNTY GOVERNMENT, FEMALE, 44

AT THE MOVIE THEATER, I ask my girlfriend if she wants popcorn and she'll say, "No, I'll just have some of yours." And I say, "No, I'll get you your own." I don't like people's hands in my popcorn. She gets mad at me when I get her her own because she just wants some of mine.

People dipping in my ketchup is no good either. I hate that. When I go out to dinner with my girlfriend or my family, instead of just pouring a little bit of ketchup on their own plate, they reach across the table and dip a french fry in my ketchup and it drives me nuts. I'll pour some ketchup into a bread plate for them so they don't continue to use mine.

ACCOUNT SPECIALIST, PUBLIC RELATIONS, MALE, 25

WHEN I GET OUT OF THE SHOWER I don't like to step on the bath mat that everyone in my family uses. I put a towel over the bath mat so I'm not stepping directly on the bath mat.

ACCOUNT EXECUTIVE, INTERNET COMPANY, FEMALE, 26

MY BATHROOM AND MY BED LINEN and towels have to be white. Other colors don't feel clean. You can't see the dirt on dark sheets or towels, so they never feel clean to me. I am very uncomfortable sleeping on dark sheets or wiping myself with a dark towel.

GRAPHIC DESIGNER, FEMALE, 32

MY MOTHER IS VERY AFRAID OF GERMS. She won't share a sandwich with us—the only way she'll try something is if she's the first to taste it. She's so afraid of germs that when she cooks, she wears latex gloves throughout the cooking and she makes sandwiches wearing the gloves. She wears the latex gloves for as long as possible during the day. The lady does not take off her gloves until she goes to bed. I rarely saw her without the latex gloves when I lived at home. If she gets any illness, I'm sure it will be from the latex that's in the gloves. That's my mom, yeah.

LAW PROFESSOR, FEMALE, AGE NOT DISCLOSED

HER MOM: CHILD PSYCHOLOGIST, 70s

I WASH THE DISHES thoroughly with soap and water before I put them in the dishwasher. I guess I don't feel that the dishwasher will clean them well enough, which is pretty stupid.

STOCKBROKER, MALE, 55

WHEN I COME HOME I don't like to track outside dirt into my apartment, so I take off my shoes and clothes in the front hall and go directly into the shower.

ADVERTISING DIRECTOR, INTERNET SALES, FEMALE, 43

MY TOOTHBRUSH and my contact lens solution are not kept in the bathroom. I keep them in a closet outside the bathroom. I once read that fecal matter bacteria can spread up to nine feet through the air. I brush my teeth in the kitchen sink and I put my contacts on in front of a mirror in the living room or bedroom. I don't use bar soap, I keep the soap in a metal dispenser. And I carry around antibacteria gel, which I use whenever I touch something.

BUSINESS PROCESS ANALYST, REAL ESTATE, FEMALE, 25

MY HUSBAND AND I share a queen-size blanket. I position the blanket so the label is always in the same corner. This way we are each always coming into contact with the same part of the blanket. In my germ-crazy mind, this seems more sanitary, even though it doesn't make sense since we are sleeping right next to each other and breathing on each other. I also cut a V-shaped notch out of the label on my pillow so I know which is my pillow and which is his pillow, so we don't mix them up. My husband isn't aware that I do this.

FLORIST, FEMALE, 52

When I travel, I put one of my clean T-shirts over the pillowcase in a hotel room and I only sleep on that pillow so I know for sure that I'm sleeping on a clean surface.

BUSINESS CONSULTANT, MALE, 22

IF SOMEONE TOUCHES MY FOOD, I won't eat it. My kids are the only exception—they're me. But no one else can touch it including my wife, my sister, or my cousin. Don't eat from my plate—I'll buy you your own!

 JR: How do you feel about eating in a restaurant, knowing that a chef may have touched it during the preparation process?
That doesn't bother me.

CLEANING MANAGER FOR OFFICE BUILDING, MALE, 39

MY FATHER-IN-LAW'S whole life revolves around gauze sponge and rubbing alcohol. He goes to the library at least once a week. When he borrows a book from the library and brings it home, before he reads the book, he will wash the plastic cover around the book with a little piece of gauze sponge and rubbing alcohol. He thinks he's doing somebody a great service by doing this.

RADIO HOST, MALE, 38

HIS FATHER-IN-LAW: PROFESSION AND AGE UNKNOWN

AT THE STARBUCKS MILK STATION, I put a napkin over the handle of the pitcher so I don't touch the handle directly when I pour milk into my coffee. I also lean against the pole in the subway as opposed to holding it.

DIRECTOR OF MARKET RESEARCH, MALE, 47

I NEVER EAT THE FRUIT or garnish on a plate because bare hands put it there. I tell myself that the rest of my food was spooned/spatulaed there. (Scary note: I put myself through school by waitressing, so I know full well what goes on in some restaurants.)

POLICY ANALYST/WRITER FOR COUNTY GOVERNMENT, FEMALE, 44

MY BROTHER-IN-LAW keeps his drink covered at all times with a plastic cover so nothing will get in it. He uses the top of a yogurt container. It doesn't matter what the beverage is or which glass or cup is used. He doesn't eat out much.

ELECTRICIAN, MALE, 34

HIS BROTHER-IN-LAW: RETIRED PARK RANGER, 45

I DON'T TOUCH doorknobs of public bathrooms. Going in, I'll push the door open, but the problem is coming out. Unless I see someone go into the bathroom, I won't go in because I know that there's no way for me to get out. If there's a paper towel, I'll grab the paper towel and use it to open the door. Sometimes I'll roll down my sleeve over my hand and open the door that way. If there are no paper towels, I'm forced to wait until someone else leaves and I follow him out the door.

PRODUCTION MANAGER, APPAREL FIRM, MALE, 64

In a restaurant, I turn the coffee cup around and hold it with the handle facing north. I then drink from the south side of the rim directly opposite the handle. My hope is that fewer mouths have come into contact with that side.

HAIR STYLIST, FEMALE, 29

I REFUSE TO DRINK out of a reusable plastic cup. I don't think plastic can be cleaned as well as glass. In a restaurant, if my beverage is served in a plastic cup, I ask for a glass or disposable paper cup instead. I'd be happiest if everything was disposable.

PROGRAMMER, CORPORATE COMMUNICATIONS DEPARTMENT, FEMALE, 40s

EVERY DAY I WASH MY DISHES in soapy water with bleach and every night I scour my sink with bleach and cleanser. I keep a bottle of bleach on my kitchen counter, which I don't dilute. At work, I don't use bleach because it would ruin my good clothes. Instead, I keep a bottle of alcohol there, which I pour on cotton swabs to wipe the phone, mouse, keyboard, computer screen, and all around my desk.

ACADEMIC, FEMALE, 52

THE BIG THING AT THE OFFICE is to have the wastebasket outside the rest rooms. People would use a paper towel to open the bathroom door to avoid germs on the door handle and then they would discard it on the floor because the wastebasket wasn't accessible. As a result, in the last five years or so, the wastebasket was moved outside the rest rooms. Since then after employees wash their hands and use the paper towel to open the door, they can drop it right into the wastebasket stationed outside the door in the hallway. I completely agree with this. Coming out of the men's room, if I discover there aren't any paper towels, I'll unbutton the cuff on my sleeve and use my sleeve to open the door. I refuse to open a door to a public rest room without something to protect my hand. This policy has even lowered the number of colds I get per year!

BUSINESS ANALYST, MALE, 39

MY COWORKER IS A GERM FREAK. When she travels and stays at a hotel, she doesn't allow her feet to come into direct contact with the floor. She wears slippers or flip-flops. She also won't directly touch the shower curtain. She uses paper towels to open and close it.

SUPERVISOR, MEDIA COMPANY RESEARCH DEPARTMENT, FEMALE, 26
HER COWORKER: MANAGER, MEDIA COMPANY RESEARCH DEPARTMENT, FEMALE, 39

WHEN I RINSE MY HAIR after I've shampooed it, I can't stand having the dirty water from my hair dripping over the rest of me so I bend over and tilt my head forward to rinse my hair. Then I straighten up and continue to clean the rest of my body.

I've been doing this since I was twelve years old and I'm twenty-five now and I can't shower any other way.

MARKETING ACCOUNT EXECUTIVE, FEMALE, 25

WHEN I FIND A COIN on the street, I pick it up with a tissue, wrap it in the tissue, and put it in my pocket until I get home. Then I wash it off with soap and water before I put it in my wallet.

FORMER MODEL, FEMALE, 70s

FOR AS LONG AS I'VE KNOWN HER, my aunt has always been extremely squeamish about germs and she takes extraordinary precautions to avoid them. All her anti-germ antics and maneuvers could fill your entire germ chapter! In a restaurant, first she wipes the chair before she sits down. Once she's seated she pours a little of the water from her water glass onto her napkin and wipes the silverware, china, and glasses before using them. Sometimes it's embarrassing because she's not always discreet about it.

ART DIRECTOR, FEMALE, 51
HER AUNT: RETIRED SEAMSTRESS, 81

MY WIFE IS VERY GERM and dirt conscious. She's Mrs. Clean. When I bring a grocery bag in from the store, it must go on the table, never on the floor. If, God forbid, the bag falls on the floor, the plastic bag is thrown out or destroyed. If an object drops on the floor or into the sink, *that's it*! Even if it wasn't touched, even if it's wrapped, it must be scrubbed, washed, sanitized. I go along with it—what else can I do?

RETIRED ADVERTISING EXECUTIVE, "EVEN MY MOTHER NEVER KNEW MY AGE"
HIS WIFE: RETIRED COLLEGE DRAMA PROFESSOR, "MY AGE IS AN UNLISTED NUMBER"

IF MY HANDS ARE DIRTY, and there's an option, I will wash them in the bathroom, not the kitchen. I know this is ridiculous because the dirt is going down the drain and I rinse the sink whether I'm using the kitchen or bathroom. I'm uncomfortable about even a remote possibility of contaminating an area where there is food.

STUDENT, MALE, 21

IN A RESTAURANT, I wrap tissues around the salt and pepper shakers and the ketchup bottle before I will pick them up. I won't touch them directly because so many people who may have had dirty hands or even licked their fingers touch them. I don't want to risk putting other people's saliva or germs on my food. Everyone else just seems to pick up these containers or bottles and not even think twice about it. Then they lick their fingers while they eat. It's disgusting—I don't see how they can live with themselves.

MEDIA SUPERVISOR, ADVERTISING, MALE, "I DON'T REVEAL MY AGE"

WHEN I STAY AT A HOTEL, I look underneath the bed in my room to make sure that nothing was left under there from previous guests. If I find something, it means that the room wasn't cleaned well enough and I won't stay in that room. I'll ask the manager to change my room. If the second one is dirty, too, then I check out.

ACCOUNT MANAGER, RETAIL, FEMALE, 54

EVER SINCE A BACTERIOLOGIST friend of my aunt's told her that food containers generate a lot of bacteria around the edges, she transfers everything into glass jars before she puts them in the refrigerator. For example, bacteria can grow in the spouts of milk cartons. Apparently glass jars don't collect as much bacteria.

INVESTMENT MANAGEMENT, BANK, MALE, 37

HIS AUNT: EXECUTIVE ASSISTANT, BANK, LATE 50s

AFTER I WASH THE DISHES with the sponge, I have to wash my hands because the sponge is filled with germs.

STUDENT, FEMALE, 20

IT'S A COMPLETE TURNOFF to see a hair, even my own, in the sink or tub or, worst of all, in food. If I am in a restaurant and I discover a hair in my food, I am revolted. I cannot finish eating and I will never set foot in that restaurant again and if I ever walk by that restaurant, I am reminded of the hair episode and it ruins my day.

BARTENDER, FEMALE, 31

AN ARTICLE I ONCE READ in a scientific journal said that the middle stalls in a public bathroom with multiple stalls have more germs because they are used more. Since then, I only use the first or last stall. If a bathroom has only two stalls then they're usually evenly used.

EDITOR, TV NEWS, FEMALE, 22

I ALWAYS KEEP MY INDEX FINGERS "clean." I think it comes from wearing contact lenses for so many years. So, if I pick up grungy stuff, I hold up my index fingers and grab the gook with my middle finger and thumb. (This is such a habit that I hardly notice. I do, however, use my index fingers for typing.)

RACONTEUR, FEMALE, 57

IF I'M EATING WITH FRIENDS or family and they want to taste my food, I will let them use the same fork as me, but after they're done I always wipe it off with a napkin or run it under a faucet. I don't want anyone's breath to taint my food.

JR: Are you concerned that you may offend someone?
> I'm discreet about it. I say, "I'll be right back, guys," and go to a faucet. They don't know where I'm going.

JR: What happens if they ask for another taste?
> I do the same routine again.

ACTOR, MALE, 22

I NEVER, NEVER, NEVER PET STRAY CATS. Why? 'Cause I don't want ringworm. Now, if I know the cat's name, I pet it and don't get ringworm. Name unknown, however—ringworm. That's what my mother told me fifty-plus years ago. Why would I run the risk of challenging this?

RACONTEUR, FEMALE, 57

I AM "GERM-A-PHOBIC" about people using my phone. When someone approaches my desk at work, I immediately go for my alcohol packets if I think they're going to use my phone.

Just before they hang up the phone, I grab the receiver from them and clean it with alcohol swabs before I hang it up. I clean my computer keys with alcohol and just about everything else. If someone borrows my pen, I wipe it with alcohol before I will use it again.

SENIOR ACCOUNT EXECUTIVE, SALES, MALE, 40

AT THE END OF A MEAL, my wife must wash any utensils or china that weren't used (as well as the dirty ones), even if they are spotlessly clean. Once it's out of the utensil drawer or cabinet, somehow it's gotten contaminated and has to be washed.

GRAPHIC ARTIST, ADVERTISING, MALE, 35
HIS WIFE: MASSAGE THERAPIST, 34

WHENEVER I PICK UP FOOD with my hands, such as a sandwich or chips, I throw away the last piece where I was holding the food. My hands may have been dirty and I don't want to eat the piece that was touching my hands. My father does that same thing, which is kind of strange. He never ate food that touched his hands either, so my germ quirk may be genetic. His excuse was that he was in the army, so his hands were always dirty. I'm careful to keep my hand in that one spot and never move my hand while I'm eating. If I have to put the food down, I make sure to pick it up in the same spot.

SYSTEMS ANALYST, COMPUTERS, PHARMACEUTICAL COMPANY, MALE, 39

I WALK UPTOWN on Second Avenue on my way to work. If it is not raining I will walk on the right-hand (east) side of the street. If it's raining I walk on the left-hand side (west). That's because I don't want dirt from buses to be swept into my face. When the bus comes downtown, if you're walking on the side where the bus stops are, it creates a wind tunnel for dirt to blow into your face. If it's raining the dirt is not as airborne as in dry weather and, therefore, the buses can't sweep the dirt up into my face.

👆 JR: That's a good tip, thank you!

SUPERVISOR, MEDIA COMPANY RESEARCH DEPARTMENT, FEMALE, 26

RESTAURANTS WITH CARPETING never seem as clean to me. It's much harder for carpeting to be kept clean than a wooden floor or tile floor or just about any other bare surface. Hairs and crumbs and dirt get embedded in the carpet and I don't think vacuuming succeeds in getting it all out, especially in places with a lot of traffic such as restaurants. Odors permeate carpets and drapes and when the odors are absorbed into carpeting and drapery, a room generally becomes stuffy. Carpeting may feel cozier to some people but it doesn't work for me. If the restaurant has carpeting, I don't eat with the same gusto.

ART DIRECTOR, FEMALE, 51

I LIKE TO READ IN BED at night before I go to sleep. When I'm finished reading and I'm about to drop off to sleep, my wife insists that I go to the bathroom to wash my hands because she thinks they are dirty from the ink in the book. My wife has a very strong sense of cleanliness.

👆 JR: Do you comply?

Sometimes. If there's something that will happen after I read the book, then I have to wash my hands.

ENERGY ECONOMIST, MALE, 52

HIS WIFE: PROFESSION AND AGE UNKNOWN

My mother loathed dirty money. She would put dollar bills between two towels and steam iron them. The steam iron removes fingerprint oil from the dollar bills. If you try it you'll see that your bills become crisp.

RADIO CALLER, MALE, PROFESSION AND AGE UNKNOWN

I WASH MY HANDS before I pee, not after. Before I pee, my hands are dirty from coming into contact with all kinds of things outside so they need to be washed. It makes much more sense to me to wash my hands before.

JR: When you meet someone after, do you shake their hand?

Absolutely!

DRIVER FOR FOREIGN CONSULATE, MALE, 44

Now I've Heard Everything!

Some folks buy a painting
Because of its style.
Some purchase a portrait
Because of its smile.
A few buy a statue
So stately and tall,
And I bought a print
For that crack in the wall.

MY MOTHER USED TO spray her hair—not just a few streaks but her entire head of hair—with theatrical hair spray to match her outfits. She would buy a case of sapphire blue, emerald green, and a lavender purple spray.

Mom was invited to a party for Texans at the White House when Lyndon Johnson was president. Mother walked into the room in a sapphire blue dress with matching sapphire blue hair and the entire room fell silent. I'm told that President Johnson—who wasn't often speechless—looked at my mother and stopped cold in his conversation. Remember, we're talking the 1960s!

Another time, a woman came up to me and said, "When I was a young girl we lived in the same neighborhood as you and I will never forget this . . . I was selling Girl Scout cookies and I knocked on your door. Your mother opened the door. She was wearing an emerald green muumuu and her hair was the exact same shade of emerald green and it wasn't St. Patrick's Day or Halloween. Your mother bent down and said, 'What can I do for you, little girl?' I screamed, wet myself, and ran all the way home."

I said, "Oh yeah, that was my mom."

 JR: Has her daughter inherited this quirk?
Well, I don't spray my hair green or purple.

HELOISE, COLUMNIST/AUTHOR/BROADCASTER, 53

HER MOTHER: INTERNATIONALLY SYNDICATED NEWSPAPER COLUMNIST HELOISE, DECEASED

WHEN I MOW THE LAWN, I mow it backward. In other words, instead of pushing it, I pull it because I want to mow over my footprints. The only thing that's left on the lawn when

I'm done mowing are the wheel tracks from the lawn mower. After I mow the lawn, I don't allow my wife or my kids on the lawn until the lines start to fade, in about forty-eight hours. Then they can play on the lawn.

☞ JR: You must be a perfectionist?
  Yes.

DIRECTOR, TRADE MARKETING, COSMETICS, MALE, 34

AS I READ THE NEWSPAPER, I rip out each page I've read and throw it away as soon as I can. I like to read the easiest pages first and eliminate those so I think I'm making progress and gathering momentum. I glance at the stock market pages and rip those pages out. I eliminate the house and home pages because I'm not interested in those. I discard the entertainment section because it's filled with movie ads, which I don't read. I'm not by nature a materialistic person, so I trash most ads. Boom, bam, I rip it out, those pages are gone. If I didn't rip the pages out and throw them away, I wouldn't know as easily what I've read and what I haven't.

☞ JR: I see you have a few newspaper pages. Why haven't you thrown them out?
  These are the nine pages, front and back, that I have left to read—some people would count it as eighteen. I like to have an optimistic attitude, so I'm glad I'm down to nine pages.

FORMER LAWYER, MALE, 60

MY METHOD OF IRONING a pair of pants is to lift up the mattress, spread the pants out, and lower the mattress on top of it.

DOORMAN, MALE, 46

WHEN I COME DOWNTOWN from the Bronx and get to mid-town Manhattan, I don't like to walk north. I'll walk east, west, and south. If I have to head north, I'll walk a few blocks east and one block north and then east and north again. I don't go straight north. I think it's because I was headed south to begin with when I came down from the Bronx. I want to continue in the same direction. Going north, I just feel like I'm backtracking.

LIBRARIAN, FEMALE, 46

I ADD UP THE NUMBERS on license plates. For example, if I see the number 816, I will add 8 + 1 = 9 + 6 = 15. The more uneven the numbers are, the happier I am.

PARALEGAL, FEMALE, 26

My mother's garbage looks like it was gift-wrapped. It's double bagged, folded over the top, taped, and then tied with string. It looks like a care package. It's a full-time occupation packing the stuff up.

PHYSICIAN, FEMALE, 48
HER MOTHER: RETIRED, 77

THE QUIRK I'm probably most well known for is my microwaving precision. I never microwave anything for a period of time divisible by five. Everyone else always microwaves for exactly one minute, or thirty or forty-five seconds, but to me that seems to unfairly favor certain numbers arbitrarily. There are numbers that seem more "right" to me than the ones that most people use, so I'll enter forty-three seconds, or two minutes sixteen seconds, or whatever other number feels like the right one. I hate the thought of a world where everything is divisible by five, so I like to think I'm evening the score a little when I use other numbers. Until a few years ago, I used prime numbers exclusively, but then I realized that was still an unbalanced approach. So now, to ensure a nice mix of numbers, I'll throw in twenty-four or fifty-eight or some other non-prime, but not-divisible-by-five number. Besides wanting to counterbalance the majority of "boring" numbers everyone else uses, I strive to make the numbers I use balance out over time with each other. One might think my efforts couldn't possibly amount to more than a mere drop in the bucket, me being just one person against a whole world of round-number microwavers, but I have a theory about that as well. I'm convinced the "rounder" numbers are less potent because of their overuse. They are so common, they pass unnoticed, but the numbers I use stand out, and that makes them strong. In my world, one forty-three more than outweighs a whole bunch of thirties. (Don't tell my high school algebra teacher that, though.)

ONE-OF-A-KIND PILLOW DESIGNER, FEMALE, 33

WHEN I'M DONE IRONING, not only do I unplug the iron, I take it a step further. I put the hot iron in the refrigerator to make sure that it doesn't ignite anything and cause a fire. Even then—I kid you not, Judy, this is how wacky it gets—when I put the iron in the refrigerator, I'll think, "What if it melts one of the soda bottles inside the refrigerator?"

RADIO BROADCASTER, MALE, 37

MY WIFE CAN'T SHUT the radio or television off mid-word. She has to wait until they've finished their thought and only then can she shut it off. If I happen to turn it off mid-word, she will turn it back on and wait for them to finish saying what they're saying and then she'll shut it off.

JR: Your wife is very polite!

VIDEO EDITOR, MALE, 31

HIS WIFE: AEROBICS INSTRUCTOR, 27

A BUSINESS ASSOCIATE deliberately built his home on a dead-end street so that as you approach the house the garage is on the far side of the house. This way he has to drive the entire length of his property to get to the garage, thereby enjoying the view. By the power of suggestion, I now take a different route home after work than I used to, so as to approach my house from its "good side."

VICE PRESIDENT, INSTITUTIONAL SALES, TEXTILES, MALE, 43

I must staple things vertically. It drives me nuts if it's horizontal.

LEGAL ASSISTANT, FEMALE, 43

I DON'T TRUST some mailboxes. If the mailbox doesn't have a schedule sheet or the schedule sheet is not filled in or if part of it is torn off, I won't use that mailbox. I prefer to mail letters near my home and, if possible, I'll hold them until I get home. There are three mailboxes near my home that I trust because letters that I've mailed in those mailboxes have never gotten lost. One of them in particular, I swear by. It's infallible.

WRITER, FEMALE, 60

MY COUSIN sends greeting cards intended for specific occasions such as a birthday or an anniversary, for entirely different occasions. For example, I just got a graduation card from him for my birthday. The card was imprinted with "Congratulations on Your Graduation." The word "graduation" was crossed out and he wrote "birthday" over it. This is his way of rebelling against card companies for forcing people to buy cards for all kinds of silly occasions.

VETERINARIAN, MALE, 36

HIS COUSIN: COMPUTER TECHNICIAN, 32

MY NINETY-THREE-YEAR-OLD grandmother has a quirk that we all talk about, but she doesn't know it. Last Memorial Day, my parents drove her seventy-five miles to visit the cemetery where some of our family is buried and to visit some friends. They spent the day at that town. The very second she got in the car to return home, Grandma got her keys out of her purse. She put her finger through the key ring, with the keys in her palm, and *jingled them all the way home!*—an hour and a half drive! My parents went stir-crazy, but they never said anything to her. (Jokingly, I'm surprised my grandmother lived to make it all the way home!) It doesn't matter where she's going. On the way home from anywhere, out come the keys . . . *jingle jingle jingle!*

BUSINESS ANALYST, MALE, 40

EVERY TIME I READ A BOOK, I smell it just to get personal with the book. You become part of the book. One time right after college I flipped open a book and it smelled good. That's when I started smelling books.

CORPORATE ACCOUNT MANAGER, TELECOMMUNICATIONS, MALE, 36

MY HUSBAND has to line everything up facing north. The silverware on the table must be facing north. When we go camping, the tent must be facing north. The bed must be facing north. He says if it's facing north, it's straight.

JR: What if the silverware in a restaurant is not facing north?

He changes seats.

RADIO CALLER, FEMALE, PROFESSION AND AGE UNKNOWN

MY COWORKER, Larry, won't leave in the morning until his watch tells him to leave. Until he hears a double beep on his watch, which signifies that it's 6:45 A.M., he will not go out of the house—not one second earlier. That's Larry.

JR to Reader: Larry confirmed this.

EXECUTIVE RECRUITER FOR TECHNOLOGY INDUSTRY, MALE, 50s

LARRY: EXECUTIVE RECRUITER FOR TECHNOLOGY INDUSTRY, MALE, 55

I ONLY LIKE to read the newspaper if it hasn't been read by anyone else. At work, if someone asks to read my paper, I will grudgingly say yes, but I'm not happy about it. I'll hand it over with the proviso that it has to be returned perfectly neat and folded and in the right order. It irks me if it looks like someone's read it. This quirk is in our genes—my sister's kind of weird about it too. Growing up, we weren't allowed to touch the paper before my father read it. I read all the sections in order, although I do like to save the special sections like the dining or weekend sections for last.

SCRIPT SUPERVISOR, FILM BUSINESS, FEMALE, 48

WHEN I HAVE DINNER at somebody's house or if I'm staying for the weekend, wherever I sat down the first time is where I always want to sit each time I visit. That's my spot and no one can sit there.

RETIRED UNIVERSITY ADMINISTRATOR, FEMALE, 65

ON THE WAY TO WORK there's a fragment of a metal tire rim embedded in the middle lane of the New Jersey Turnpike near the exit where I get off. It's imperative that I drive over it. Once I've driven over it, I have to make a very fast lane switch. It adds an element of danger and excitement to my morning commute. I don't really believe in good luck as much as bad luck. If I don't do it or if I'm forced to miss my exit because there's an eighteen-wheeler right there, a bunch of bad things are going to happen. I've been doing this as long as I noticed that it was there, which is now about seven years.

EMERGENCY PHYSICIAN, MALE, 53

AT A NEWSSTAND, if I want to browse through a magazine, even if I have no intention of buying it, I will still take one from the middle or back and not from the front because I don't want to browse through one that may be used.

COMPUTER PROGRAMMER, MALE, 27

I WILL FREQUENTLY estimate the time it will take to get from where I am to my destination and then count seconds or minutes to myself to see whether I'm right. For example, let's say that I think it will take about twenty seconds from the time that I get into the elevator on the ground floor of my apartment building to get to my floor, walk to my door, unlock the door, get inside my apartment, and lock the door. When I step into the elevator I'll begin counting backward . . . twenty, nineteen, eighteen, and so on. I put pressure on myself. If I see that I'm over or under time, I'll slow up or speed up the counting. Another example: If I'm riding the subway from 14th Street to 42nd Street, I give myself an approximation of how long it should take to pull into the station. If I think it's going to take thirty seconds, again, I start counting backward thirty, twenty-nine, twenty-eight, et cetera. If I get the feeling that I'm going to be off, I start slowing down and when I get to one, before I reach zero, I'll hold my breath until the train gets into the station. Sometimes I'll think, "This is stupid," and I'll continue breathing and forget about the whole thing.

LAWYER, MALE, 55

I'm in sales and if I'm having a slow day, I'll beep myself, hoping that it will open the floodgate for more sales.

SALES, PRINTING AND GRAPHICS, MALE, 34

WHEN I TAKE NOTES it has to be in rainbow colors—blue, red, purple, pink, and yellow. I'm more interested in reading it and I retain the information better when it's more colorful. I switch colors as I take notes. There's no special order as long as it's different colors. When I use rainbow colors, I usually get an A on the exam.

INSURANCE SALES, FEMALE, 22

I NEED TO KISS my girlfriend in combinations of two or five kisses. I'll give her two kisses on the left and then she'll kind of go for a third but I'll turn my head to stop her so she'll end up kissing me on my cheek. If I know that it will extend to five kisses, then I'll go to five and turn my head then. I'm a person who always likes to even things out. If I kiss her on her forehead, I need to kiss her on her chin and you can go from there . . .

WEB DEVELOPER, MALE, 32

I THINK I INHERITED this from my mom—I never throw out aluminum foil. I must wash it and reuse it again and again, no matter how rumpled up or disgusting it is. I realize this is nuts.

OWNER, GARMENT CENTER BUSINESS, FEMALE, 40s

MY FRIEND SITS at the light and has to clean the dust out of the car vents with a little paintbrush. His psychiatrist advised him to do this.

HOUSEWIFE, FEMALE, 51

HER FRIEND: MANAGING DIRECTOR, 35

WHEN I'M WALKING down the street with a long, pointy umbrella, I can't help but put it into the cracks in the sidewalk and dig it in there. Frequently, it gets stuck and slips out of my hand and when I walk back to retrieve it, it's standing up straight in between the sidewalk squares. I don't allow myself to miss a single crack without digging it in there. If I miss one it ruins the whole walk.

JR: It must take a long time to get to your destination.
    Definitely.

ADVERTISING SALESPERSON, INTERNET INDUSTRY, MALE, 26

I HAVE AN IRRATIONAL HATRED of fonts that don't close on themselves all the way (meaning the loops don't touch the stems on letters like b, p, d, e, et cetera). They seem lazy and unfinished, like they don't take their jobs seriously. This carries over to my handwriting as well. If I'm jotting down a note, and one of the letters doesn't connect all the way, I have to go back and make it connect, preferably so that it's not obvious it's even been corrected. Otherwise, I feel my thought isn't complete.

ONE-OF-A-KIND PILLOW DESIGNER, FEMALE, 33

NO MATTER what station I'm listening to on the radio, I have to turn to WPLJ, 95.5, before I shut it off. Sometimes I have to start from WPLJ, but I always have to end with WPLJ.

ASSISTANT, EQUITY RESEARCH DEPARTMENT, FEMALE, 24

WHEN I FILL MY CAR with gas at a gas station, I always have to make certain that the meter ends on the number five no matter what. I've done this for years. I wouldn't dream of leaving without it ending on a five.

DENTAL HYGIENIST, FEMALE, 33

QUITE OFTEN, before my friend goes through a doorway or sits down, he spins his body around clockwise once and only then will he go through the door or sit down. I finally noticed that he does this when he has to make a left turn. If it's impossible to approach a chair from the right, he spins. One day I asked him, "Why do you do this?" He said, "I'm right-handed but it has nothing to do with that—I always try to do the right thing so I never make a left turn. Right is the right way; going to the right is going in the right direction." When he approaches a chair from the left, he spins to the right to compensate. I asked him what he does at an intersection when he has to make a left turn. He said, "Three rights make a left." I said, "You're out of your mind." If possible, he moves the chair but many times you don't have a choice. It's bizarre.

CHIEF INFORMATION OFFICER, TECHNOLOGIST FOR TRADING FIRM, MALE, 38

HIS FRIEND: PROGRAMMER, 25

MY CATS' NAMES are Lucas and Elliot and I have to pet each of them the same amount of times because they get upset if I give one more attention than the other. If I spend five minutes with one, I have to spend five minutes with the other one. If I pat one and the other one is not around, I have to go looking for him. I'm now conditioned to do it.

ELECTRICAL ENGINEER, MALE, 29

LUCAS: 3 1/2

ELLIOT: 2

SOMETIMES I SEE how far I can go up the steps to the first landing of my building before the door slams shut. I try to see if I can beat my previous record. I usually get to a certain step. If I'm feeling very vigorous, I get a little further. If I'm carrying packages, I won't reach that step. It's a little game I play.

GRAPHIC DESIGNER, MALE, 52

WHEN I CLOSE my locker at the gym, if any other lockers in the same row are open and no one's looking, I close them all. It's bad luck if I don't.

CAR SALESMAN, MALE, 47

MY HOME IS A DISASTER but my car is immaculate, inside and out. When it comes to putting things away, I'm completely disorganized. The clean laundry will stay in the basket for a week before I put it away, but the car is spotless. I wash my car once a week and I polish it every month or two. I'm fanatical about it. I'm a car guy. I have several old cars that I take care of—an old Cadillac, a little sports car. It's a passion; maybe that's part of it. I neglect my personal stuff, but the car must be in order. The garage is a disaster too. I enjoy fixing the car, but it takes me a month to put the tools away after I'm done. I need somebody to follow me around and pick up after me.

REAL ESTATE APPRAISER, MALE, 32

I'M A WRITER and I buy spiral notebooks to write in. If I'm not satisfied with the first few sentences or paragraphs that I write in a new notebook, then I've got to throw the whole notebook away and buy a new one.

 JR: Why?

Because it's wrong. It's tainted. There's something awful about it.

 JR: Can't you just rip out those pages?

No, because then there aren't as many pages as in a new notebook.

WRITER, MALE, 38

MY WIFE AND I have been married a long time—over fifty years. We exchange cards at least three times a year for various occasions such as birthdays, anniversaries, and Valentine's Day. We don't sign or date the cards. We usually put it out on the table the night before. Although we've been following this ritual the entire time we've been married, we both act surprised and say, "Ohhhhhhhh!" About ten years went by like this when I began to realize that her cards looked familiar. I didn't say anything about it. That birthday card would come and I thought to myself, "Gee, I think I got that before." Anniversary card, "That sure looks familiar." One time, I turned the card around and checked the price. I was paying about $2.75 for a card and her card cost 35¢, that's how old it was! I go out and buy a beautiful new card every year and hers is a rerun. I don't mind and I really can't complain about it. During the early years she was home with the kids. It was much easier for me to get out and shop. Besides, we're saving money!

JR: Does she think you don't notice?
I once said, "I recognize this card!" She said, "Oh my!" She knows—we just play the game.

RETIRED ADVERTISING EXECUTIVE, "EVEN MY MOTHER NEVER KNEW MY AGE"

HIS WIFE: RETIRED COLLEGE DRAMA PROFESSOR, "MY AGE IS AN UNLISTED NUMBER"

I CHANGE MY VOICE MAIL at work every morning and I purposely record the next day's date even though it's the wrong date. The reason I do that is to see if people are paying attention. Nine out of ten times nobody says anything. Every once in a while someone will say, "Hey, moron, it's the third." My wife controls the answering machine at home.

SALESMAN, MALE, 36

It irks my mother when the number of windows on the front of a house doesn't add up to an even number.

GRAPHIC DESIGNER, MALE, 36

HIS MOTHER: RETIRED, 64

THERE ARE TWO ELEVATORS in our high-rise but my roommate will only take the elevator on the left. When she pushes the button, if the right elevator comes before the left elevator, then she will take the stairs up to the eighth floor. One of her excuses is that she needs the exercise.

FREELANCE JOURNALIST, MALE, 26

HIS ROOMMATE: HEAD OF TECH SUPPORT AT A UNIVERSITY, 28

ON ANY EXAM or questionnaire, I begin with the last question first and work my way forward. I review the instructions on the first page, then immediately go to the last question. It's just more comfortable for me. I do better.

SPECIAL EVENTS COORDINATOR, FEMALE, 25

WHEN WALKING THROUGH my parents' house, I take an even number of steps on each different surface (six times on the dining room carpet, twice on the entryway tile, four times on the entryway rug, twice on the entryway tile, eight times on the hallway carpet . . .). Walking even times across each surface is not confined to my parents' house—it just has a lot more surfaces than my apartment for explanation purposes. There's an area of tile between the rug and carpet that's big enough for only one step, so I have to drag the toe of the other foot just so I can technically have two feet down. I'm convinced that most of us have these rhythms that we follow subconsciously and often don't even notice. Recently I became aware that when I'm applauding I almost always use nine claps. I've noticed similar things in others, too.

MBA STUDENT, MALE, 26

ALL MY STUFFED ANIMALS must be sitting up or lying face up. Otherwise they may get smothered and they won't be able

to see what's going on or play with me. They have their own
separate bed in the spare room. At the moment I have about
eight of them.

ADMINISTRATIVE CLERK, FEMALE, 51

WHEN MY FRIEND and her family drive over a bridge and get
to the middle of the bridge, they all look up and tap the roof of
the car for good luck.

JR: Has she been having good luck?
Yes, she has.

QUALITY ASSURANCE ANALYST, POSTAL SERVICE, FEMALE, 48

WHEN I'M RUNNING on the treadmill, my cat jumps on the
treadmill and runs with me. I don't know why. I don't ask him
to. He just does. He runs right next to me and stays there the
entire time I'm running.

JR: You must have a very fit cat.
My daughters say that the cat is in better shape than I am.

RETIRED FIREMAN, 66

I WILL NOT MOVE the car until . . . one, everybody has their
seatbelt on, two, all doors are locked, and three, I sing half of
the song, "The Wheels on the Bus Go Round and Round." Then
I know I'll have a safe ride.

RADIO BROADCASTER, MALE, 37

EVERY DAY I MAKE A LIST of things to do when I get into
work and I do them in the order in which I wrote them. I
check them off with a little X when I get it done. If I do it out of

order, it will throw me off and make me feel that I'm not on schedule. Also, at the beginning of the year I fill in every weekday, Monday to Friday, on the calendar with about six or seven things that I have to do to start the day as soon as I walk in the office. I have to check my e-mail. I have to check the attendance of the workers. It gets my day off to a good start and gives me the feeling that I've accomplished something right off the bat.

MANAGER, SECURITY, TELEPHONE COMPANY, MALE, 56

I can't sit in a room unless the door is closed. If it's half open I have to close it.

E-COMMERCE CONSULTANT, MALE, 25

I TAKE OUT MY MECHANICAL PENCIL in the morning when I get to work and never let go of it. I hold onto it all day long no matter what I'm doing, whether I'm using it or not. If for some reason I don't have that pencil in my hand, I'm just lost. I cannot do anything unless I have my pencil. I will walk around the office until I find it. When it has to be replaced, I don't have to get the same one but the new one then becomes my pencil until it dies.

CFO, INTERNET COMPANY, FEMALE, 37

IF THE STREET has even slabs with cracks, I pay attention to whether I get four or five paces in between each crack.

EXECUTIVE RECRUITER, MALE, 31

THE DRIVEWAY to my house is circular, so I can go either to the left or to the right to get to the main road. Each and every single time, when I back out of my driveway, I go to the right. I don't know why. Perhaps it's because I'm right-handed. When I come in, I can go either way but, again, I always make that first right.

MANAGER OF A DATA ENTRY AREA, MALE, 42

MY HUSBAND buys two copies of the same book because he wants to keep one copy neat and clean for his library. He buys many books because he reads a lot. He buys certain books for aesthetic reasons because he thinks they're beautiful books. He only buys one of those because he doesn't actually read those. They are put on the shelf for show. You cannot move it. He will immediately notice if you've changed its position. We've tested him. He buys a separate copy for me because my books look read. We have separate bookcases. He has a library for the books that he reads and another one for the beautiful books. They are in two separate locations in the house. He also has a personal seal, which he stamps on the first page of each of his books in the lower right corner. He wants to separate them from mine, which really isn't necessary because you can tell immediately which are mine and which are his. Even the ones that he's read look brand new. The seal says, "The Library of" and his name. He also keeps the register receipts for the book somewhere inside the book. Needless to say, the receipt is also in pristine condition. He's trying to teach our daughter to keep the books neat, but I think she got my genes.

ANALYST, NATIONAL BANK, FEMALE, 31

HER HUSBAND: SELF-EMPLOYED, WHOLESALE BUSINESS, 46

NOBODY CAN TOUCH my computer either at home or in the office. I feel very strongly about this. It's almost like my pet—I'm very possessive about it. Sometimes my sons come over to the house and they start playing with it and it gets me nuts. For some reason, people have a habit of rearranging the icons or changing the way the screen looks. It's my possession—it has to be the way I want it.

PRODUCTION MANAGER, APPAREL FIRM, MALE, 64

I WON'T CROSS THE STREET until I absolutely have to, until I feel there's a sign to cross to the other side. Sometimes the sign is an attractive woman, but other times it's a special break in the traffic or something similar.

 **JR: Are you frequently late?**

I don't have to cross at a certain moment. During a journey I know that eventually I must cross the street but I won't do it until something guides me over.

ARCHITECT, MALE, 32

WHEN I WAS IN ELEMENTARY SCHOOL someone asked me if I had a pet peeve and I said no, so I decided to develop one. The rabbit ears on books—those little folded-over corners— drive me nuts, so that became my pet peeve. Even if it takes me an hour, I go through the entire book and I unfold each one.

ATTORNEY, MALE, 25

THE VOLUME on the television has to be on an even number not divisible by 10 or 11. The closest I can get to explaining the logic behind this is that I like even numbers but I don't like "boring" even numbers (the same number twice in a row or a number ending in a zero). This gets especially problematic when the ideal volume is in the low 20s: 20 and 22 are off limits, 18 is too quiet, and 24 is too loud. Seventeen used to be acceptable when it was the channel number for ESPN, and 51 (though seldom used) is acceptable because it is the jersey number of my hero Willie McGee.

MBA STUDENT, MALE, 26

WHEN I'M WALKING with somebody, I have to be to their right because if there's nobody on my left side I feel empty. If they are to the right of me, I will rearrange myself and go around them.

ADMINISTRATIVE ASSISTANT, FEMALE, 29

IF MY FATHER makes a list of things he has to do during the day, instead of just crossing out or checking off the chore he finished, he'll write an entirely new list with that chore eliminated. He's very anal.

COLLEGE STUDENT, MALE, 22

HIS FATHER: BAIL BONDSMAN, 42

BOTH SCREWS in all my light switch plates must be aligned exactly vertically or horizontally. They must match. They cannot be diagonal because it's hard to have both of them at exactly the same angle.

 JR: What about the screws in other things?

If there is more than one screw in an object, I like them to be aligned but the screws in other objects aren't as noticeable. Light switches are used frequently, whenever a light is turned on or off, so they're much more noticeable. It's a very important thing to align screws!

MANAGING DIRECTOR, REAL ESTATE, MALE, 47

I ONLY LIKE ODD NUMBERS. If I'm shaking salt or pepper into something I'm cooking, I'll shake it or grind it an odd number of times. I noticed this about thirty years ago when I started to cook seriously. Another example is that I can never buy a half dozen or a dozen flowers, it has to be seven or thirteen.

JR: Will the shopkeeper make an exception for you?

Yes, they always cut me a deal—sometimes they throw the seventh or thirteenth one in for free.

ASSISTANT REFERENCE LIBRARIAN, FEMALE, 62

IF I WANT TO APPLY LIPSTICK and I don't have a mirror, I look at the top of the lipstick cap while I'm applying the lipstick. Although it doesn't have a mirror and is not reflective, if I focus on it, I feel like I can see my lips without actually seeing them. It allows me to center myself and I can apply the lipstick perfectly.

ARTIST/PAINTER, FEMALE, "MIDDLE-AGED"

When I walk on the sidewalk, I can't walk directly behind people over their footsteps because I don't want to take on any of their bad karma or get bad heebee jee-bees from them. I try to zigzag behind them.

TV COMMERCIAL EDITOR, MALE, 29

THE MEN IN OUR FAMILY put the car into neutral, out of gear, so they can coast going down a hill. They'll just let it coast until the speed slows to about thirty miles per hour before they'll touch the gas pedal again.

HOUSEWIFE, FEMALE, 31

I HAVE FIVE LAUNDRY BAGS, but it doesn't matter how many laundry bags I have because I always use a black plastic garbage bag for laundry. I keep my laundry in them and bring my laundry to the Laundromat in them. I don't like using laundry bags despite the fact that they're very convenient because they have a strap. People keep on giving them to me and I bought two because I thought I'd change once I moved to the city from Canada, but I still use garbage bags.

MANAGER OF COMMERCE PROGRAMS, INTERNET COMPANY, MALE, 25

IN ELEMENTARY SCHOOL, I did well on standardized tests, but it wasn't because I was giving my undivided attention to the test itself. It was more important what the answer choices represented. My answer form depicted an athletic contest between A (Kareem Abdul-Jabar), B (Larry Bird), C (Vince Coleman or Steve Carlton), and D (Abner Doubleday, the mythical inventor of baseball). I paid attention to what was being asked in the test, but I also paid close attention to which answer choice was "winning."

MBA STUDENT, MALE, 26

I HEAR A SONG or series of musical notes, even sirens or other sounds, in numbers. I assign consecutive numbers from one to eight to the notes of the musical scale. Do is one, re is two, mi is three, et cetera. One is the darkest color and eight is the lightest color. A song playing in a movie can be a darker color, maybe somebody's eyes, one; hair, if it's blond, is eight. I can't help it anymore. They taught me this in school and now it's an obsession.

RECEPTIONIST/MUSICIAN, FEMALE, 31

I NEVER MAKE RESERVATIONS for a hotel, restaurant, or anything else when I travel, no matter where I go or how far I go. I'm afraid that I won't have fun if I make reservations beforehand. I've gone to America, Marrakesh, Bangkok—all over the world. I just show up. I never bring more than I can carry. When I arrive, I start looking for a place by asking around. I've ended up going home with cab drivers and staying at their place.

GRAPHIC DESIGNER, MALE, 26

MY FAVORITE NUMBER IS TWELVE. If I see thirty-six, I think of how to make it twelve in my head. I'll divide it by three. If I see the number two, I'll multiply it by six to make it twelve. Or I doodle the number twelve.

ADMINISTRATIVE ASSOCIATE, FEMALE, 33

A WOMAN I WORK WITH insists on walking on the left side of anyone she's walking with. She said that she feels "off balance" if she doesn't walk on the left. She said that she'd walk on the right just as long as someone shorter than her walks on her left. (Connie is only five feet one inch tall).

BUSINESS ANALYST, MALE, 39

HIS COLLEAGUE: BUSINESS ANALYST, 40

WHEN I READ A MAGAZINE, I open it right to left and read the last page first because there's usually something very interesting on the last page. Once I'm back there, I start flipping through the magazine from the back.

TEACHER, FEMALE, 38

I READ CATALOGS back to front. I don't want to be manipulated by the catalog publisher's ideas of what I should see first.

ONE-OF-A-KIND PILLOW DESIGNER, FEMALE, 33

I READ MAGAZINES backward, starting with the back cover. Back to front seems to be a more natural hand movement for a right-handed person. I'm right-handed. It feels awkward to go in the correct direction.

BROADCAST TRAFFIC COORDINATOR, FEMALE, 28

ALTHOUGH I LIVE AND WORK in a digital world, I use nondigital "technology" for the storage, searching, and retrieval of my data. I'm a serial hard-copy filer. I keep papers in a stack or in a loose-leaf binder and I find what I want by determining the approximate date that I received it and evaluating how deep it is in the stack or the loose-leaf. I estimate the level where I think items with that date are. I find information by when I received that information, not by what type of information it is. If I want to find someone's phone number, I don't find it in an address book, I find it by the date I met that person. If it's too far back to remember, it's probably not important to me anyway.

JR: Don't you find this time-consuming?

No, it's much faster than other types of filing. I usually find information before other people do, as my colleagues can attest. In business school, I was made fun of because most people kept categories of every class and every subject and I just had one bag that I always carried with me with everything in it.

PRESIDENT, INTERNET SOFTWARE FOR SCHOOLS COMPANY, MALE, 36

I CAN'T HAVE ANYTHING in my pockets when I drive. I have to remove my keys, cell phone, wallet, and anything else and they all go in various designated spots in the car. The cell phone goes next to the emergency brake, the wallet goes into the center console, and anything else in my pocket goes into the glove compartment. If they're in my pocket, it changes the whole driving experience.

MANAGER, BIKE STORE, MALE, 22

I MUST HAVE TISSUES on me at all times, whether I'm in my house or outside. Even if I'm wearing a robe or pajamas, they must be with me. I guess I'm anticipating the nonexistent nosebleed, running nose, potential cold. People know I'm "The Tissue Man." They know that they can come to me if they need one. I feel naked without them. If I were a streaker, I'd be naked except for a little pouch with tissues.

RETIRED, MALE, 72

I FOLLOW THE EXACT SAME ROUTE to and from work. For four years now I cross the street in exactly the same place.

 JR: Don't you get bored?

No, because my mind can go to a different place and my body just knows where it's going.

OFFICE MANAGER, MALE, 39

WHENEVER I'M IN SOMEONE ELSE'S CAR I always fiddle with the car stereo to make sure that their treble and balance and bass are the way I like it to be. Some people get upset, others don't mind. I know I'm doing them a favor.

WRITER/JOURNALIST, MALE, 31

WHENEVER I'M ON A PLANE and it's landing—from the moment I feel that the wheels are down and it's about to land on the runway—I have to hold my breath until the plane hits the ground and only then can I stop holding my breath. That way the plane will land safely.

ADMINISTRATIVE ASSOCIATE, HUMAN RIGHTS ORGANIZATION, FEMALE, 21

IF I SEE A DIGITAL CLOCK I always add up the digits. If it's 3:15 A.M., I'll add it up and think nine. It's especially satisfying if it's a multiple of ten—I'll wait for the minute to come. Sometimes I'll add up telephone numbers and addresses and license plates, but mainly clocks.

MEDICAL STUDENT, MALE, 30

I LIKE TO DECORATE my home so that it looks the best that it can look and once it's decorated to perfection, I need to redecorate. This occurs about every six months. I rearrange my furniture in every possible configuration to see all the ways that it can look.

TECHNICAL RECRUITER, FEMALE, 25

A FRIEND OF MINE has a thing with the number three. He hates three. You cannot do anything to him three times. Two is okay but if you tap him three times, he'll ask you to tap him again. If a girl kisses him three times, it has to be four times, no matter what. However awkward it will be for him to say, "Kiss me again," he will say it.

ASSISTANT EDITOR, MALE, 21

HIS FRIEND: PROFESSION AND AGE UNKNOWN

I NEVER TURN the ceiling fan on anywhere regardless of the heat because I'm afraid it will fly off and decapitate me.

MARKETING CONSULTANT, FEMALE, 42

WHEN I SIT DOWN to watch television to relax and I see the light on in the bathroom or kitchen or any room within my vision, I have to get up to turn it off. I've been doing this for forty-six years.

 JR: Why?

Growing up, my father would say, "If you're not in the room, turn the light off."

 JR: Are you trying to save on electricity?

Not one bit.

SCHOOL BUS DRIVER, MALE, 46

WE COUNT VOLKSWAGEN BEETLES whenever we see them in the street. It's a game to see who counts the most of each color during the course of the day. So far today, I've seen two silvers, one red, and three blue ones. I always give the yellows away because I don't like that color.

HOMEMAKER, FEMALE, 40

WHEN I LEAVE REMINDER voice mail messages for myself, I always say, "Hi, it's me" and "Bye."

POLICY ANALYST/WRITER FOR COUNTY GOVERNMENT, FEMALE, 44

I WON'T WALK on subway grates or wooden folding trap doors—anything where there's a cellar underneath or where I can see an empty space underneath that I can fall into.

ARTIST, FEMALE, 42

I HAVE TO PROGRAM the radio station from the lowest station to the highest, left to right. I'm from Philadelphia, so I start with 93.3 all the way up to 106.1, in order. I don't like anybody touching my car radio when I'm driving. I'm the only one who can play with the radio. If someone else plays with it I'll give them a little smack on the hand like, "You're bad—don't touch my radio ever again!"

ACCOUNT SPECIALIST, PUBLIC RELATIONS, MALE, 25

IF I SIT DOWN at a computer, whether it's mine or someone else's, I will reset the keyboard repeat rate to the fastest setting because I hate waiting. When I hold down the space bar or the up or down arrows, I want them to move rapidly.

 JR: When you leave do you change it back?

No, it's in the best interest of that person to have it at the faster rate.

STRATEGIST, INTERNET START-UP COMPANY, MALE, 28

When I can't avoid stepping in a puddle of water, I have to get the soles of both of my shoes wet, otherwise I feel "uneven."

POLICY ANALYST/WRITER FOR COUNTY GOVERNMENT, FEMALE, 44

I LIKE EVEN NUMBERS. I don't like odd numbers, so if I buy apples or if I take jelly beans, it has to be an even amount. Instead of taking one, I'll take two. My husband thinks it's crazy and he sometimes tries to give me just one of something and I'm like, "No, no—you have to give me another one!" I think I just like things in pairs. I don't like one thing to be left out.

MARKETING ANALYST, FEMALE, 33

MY ROOMMATE likes to do what he calls "harvesting his toenails." Instead of cutting his toenails every two or three weeks, he cuts them every three to four months or six months. He lets them grow nice and long and then he cuts them and puts them all in this case that he made out of a Dr Pepper can. It's sort of like a piggy bank. He collects all of his toenails in there and saves them. He advertises this to people and says that if you start doing it, you realize that it's a good thing to do. Even with his socks on, he scrapes his toenails against the carpeting.

MANAGEMENT CONSULTANT, MALE, 23
HIS ROOMMATE: STUDENT, 22

WHEN I LEAVE MY APARTMENT I make a mental note about where I've left the remote control, so I don't have to go looking around for it when I return.

BANKER, MALE, 29

I LIVE BY MYSELF, but I close the door behind me everywhere I go in my apartment. When I go to the bathroom, I close the door for the sake of privacy, but there's no one else around. I sleep with my bedroom door closed. There's no reason to do that. I recently graduated from college, so I'm accustomed to living in dorms and group housing. Closing the door every-

where you went was the only way you could get any privacy.
I'm still in that mode even though I live by myself now.

BUSINESS CONSULTANT, MALE, 22

IF A PENCIL is missing an eraser or if the eraser is worn down
to the metal that it's surrounded by, no matter how new or
lovely the pencil is, it's garbage. No eraser, no pencil.

APPAREL SALESMAN, MALE, 48

IF I'M WATCHING a sporting event on TV and I'm rooting for
one of the teams in the contest, I have to flip away from the
station I'm watching and flip back during commercials an
even number of times. So if a commercial starts, I change the
station, see what else is on, and flip back. I have to do that one
more time, or else the team I am rooting for will start playing
poorly. Exception: If the team I'm rooting for is playing poorly,
I have to flip around and back an odd number of times to
change my team's fortunes.

MBA STUDENT, MALE, 26

MY FRIEND has a very hairy cat and the way she controls the
cat hair is to suck it off with a vacuum cleaner.

ART HANDLER (MOVES AND TAKES CARE OF ART FOR MUSEUMS AND GALLERIES), MALE, 31

HIS FRIEND: STORE MANAGER, 31

I HAVE TO HAVE two or more errands to do before I go out.
I'm probably an over-organized human being. What can you do
to help me?

RETIRED TRADE SHOW ORGANIZER, MALE, 66

IN WASHINGTON, D.C., there's a homeless man who's popularly known as Moses. There have been articles written about him. He stands on New York Avenue under a highway overpass and greets morning and evening rush hour traffic by waving a branch up and down. Some have speculated that this is a Christian type of cross maneuver but I think it's just a greeting and a goodwill blessing as people come and go to and from the city. I purposely went that way every day when I was commuting to work despite the fact that it was less convenient and took longer. I knew that it would be a good day if Moses was there and it would be a bad day if he wasn't. I just wanted to see it and be a part of it.

MANAGEMENT CONSULTANT, MALE, 23

EACH TIME AS I GO over a bridge or through a tunnel, I keep on saying to myself, "Thank God. Thank God. Thank God." This ensures that I will get to the other end safely. I also like to build up my "Thank Gods" and have them in reserve for other occasions when I forget to say it.

SALESPERSON, PRINTING, MALE, 62

WHEN I GET HOME at night, before I can begin to relax I have to go into the hallway and straighten out the tassels on both ends of our two Oriental rugs. It restores order to the house.

SENIOR MANAGEMENT, DATABASE MARKETING, MALE, 46

I'M RELUCTANT to have my voice recorded because I'm convinced that I will be famous one day and I don't want anything to come back and haunt me. In fact, I'm surprised that I'm not already famous despite the fact that I don't have any special skills or talent or anything about me that would lead to fame.

DIRECTOR OF SALES, PUBLISHING, FEMALE, 30

IF I WANT TO DISCARD a piece of paper, I wad it up and throw it toward the garbage can like a basketball shot. If I miss, I won't just pick it up and throw it in. No—I will walk over; pick up the piece of paper; go back to the spot where I threw it from; and keep trying until I make the shot. That's where two hours of my workday goes because I keep missing it!

RADIO HOST, MALE, 35

WHEN I PLAYED SPORTS in high school, before any game or meet, I repeated everything I did in the morning six times because six is my lucky number. I would do things like turn off the water in the shower six times, step out of the shower six times, and wave my arms six times.

JR: How did you do in the sports?
Pretty well, actually.

STUDENT, SENIOR, 21

I DON'T USE SPEED DIAL on my cell phone or my phone at home. I force myself to dial the number every single time. This way I'll remember them.

COMPUTER PROGRAMMER, MALE, 27

AMERICANS WILL THINK NOTHING of sitting in an aisle seat of a bus or train even when the window seat is unoccupied. This annoys me tremendously. My way of educating the people of America to make this a better country is to look for a sleeping person sitting in an aisle seat with an empty seat next to him. I nudge him to ensure that I'll wake him up and he will have to stand up to let me in. I do this automatically on a regular basis three or four days a week. I think it shows bad attitude and inconsideration when someone makes it difficult to get an available seat. In Sweden, where I'm from, people generally try to fill the window seats first. It's much easier to load and unload a bus in Sweden when people are helping each other.

👆 JR: Are you succeeding in educating us?

On the contrary—it's getting worse every day!

ACCOUNT SUPERVISOR, PUBLIC RELATIONS, MALE, 31

WHEN WE GO TO PICK OUT a Christmas tree, my daughter always picks out the most pathetic looking tree, because she feels sorry for it and she wants to give it a home.

COMMUNICATIONS CONSULTANT, MALE, 50

HIS DAUGHTER: HOMEMAKER, 30

I TEND TO LIKE TO CHANGE radio stations in the car even when a song I like is on, but there are two songs for which I don't allow myself to touch the radio dial until they finish. I always listen to "What Becomes of the Brokenhearted" (in honor of the 1972 U.S. Olympic men's basketball team) and "Catch Us If You Can" (in honor of the 1986 St. Louis Cardinals) in their entirety. If I arrive where I'm going, I have to sit in the car until the song finishes.

MBA STUDENT, MALE, 26

WHAT I OFTEN DO is to call my cell phone several times and leave myself messages so when I look at it in the morning it says I have two or three received phone calls. I leave messages such as, "You sexy thing!" "You love yourself." "You're awesome." "Chicks love you." "You're hangin' ten." It makes me feel good about myself when I listen to my messages.

DANCE INSTRUCTOR FOR MUSIC GROUP, MALE, 29

All of my keys must be pointing in the same direction. If, God forbid, I put one on and it's facing the wrong way, I'm freaked. I have to fix it as soon as possible. I've really tried hard to ignore it, but I just can't. After a while, it has to be adjusted.

RADIO HOST, MALE, 44

EACH TIME MY NEPHEW reads a series of books, he'll read every single book in the series through the most current one. Then he'll go back to the first book and reread each book in the series again in succession to make sure he absorbed everything and nothing has gotten by him. If he still feels that he may have missed some details, he'll read it all again.

NETWORK MANAGER, COMPUTERS, MALE, 37

HIS NEPHEW: STUDENT, 15

WHEN THERE'S A FLASHING LIGHT, from an airplane in the sky, for example, I will keep trying to close my eyes when the light is at its brightest. Until I actually get it, I won't stop. It's a race-against-time game I play. I have to get it before it's not there anymore. It's something I've been doing since I was a kid and I don't know why.

DIRECTOR OF EMERGING TECHNOLOGY, COMPUTERS, MALE, 37

I HAVE TO FINISH A CHAPTER of a book before I can put it down. There has to be some sort of finale or closure before I allow myself to put a book down, no matter how tired I am or how many pages the chapter has. I can never close a book in the middle of a chapter. That's the way I read.

COLLEGE STUDENT, MALE, 20

MY FRIEND Julie counts everything she eats because she only eats in odd numbers. She'll eat seven French fries, for example, or three pieces of chocolate. She's just very funny like that.

JR: Is there a specific number for each type of food?
As long as it's an odd number, it doesn't matter. If she's taking handfuls of popcorn, for example, she'll take three handfuls. If it's bigger items like cookies, she'll make sure she has three or five.

JR: Do you have any idea why?
She hasn't given me an explanation, although I've asked her. It's the same thing at the gym. She exercises for an odd number of minutes on the machines.

EDITORIAL ASSISTANT, PUBLISHING, FEMALE, 24
HER FRIEND: PROGRAM MANAGER, PROMOTION, 24

I will not hang up the phone first. Even if I end the conversation, I need to hear the other dial tone to know that the conversation is over. I can't tell you why.

BROADCAST TRAFFIC COORDINATOR, 28

IF I'M THE LAST PERSON to leave a room and the light needs to be turned off, I don't turn it off until I'm standing completely outside that room, then I reach back inside and turn the light off.

JR: Why?
It started in my childhood and it's just continued.

INSURANCE BROKER, MALE, 23

About the Author

Judy Reiser began collecting quirks after a conversation with a friend in which they each divulged something crazy they do. After having a good laugh about it, she soon discovered that everyone seems to have quirks. She has been observing, gathering, marveling at, and laughing about quirks ever since.

You can imagine how many quirks she's acquired after interviewing over two thousand people. And she couldn't afford it—she had too many to begin with. If she had written this book as an autobiography, it would have been much longer!

Her previous book was *And I Thought I Was Crazy!*

You can learn more about Judy and her books by visiting her Web site, www.katalinmedia.com.

Quirk Quest

If you've observed a quirk or idiosyncrasy, in yourself or anyone else, that is amusing, strange, touching, or a clever idea, I'd love to hear about it. Please include as many details as possible, as well as your gender, age, and profession and the gender, age, and profession of anyone involved. Also, please provide your contact information. Mail or e-mail it to:

Judy Reiser
c/o Andrews McMeel Publishing
4520 Main Street
Kansas City, MO 64111-7701
jreiser@katalinmedia.com

I eat my peas with honey,
I've done it all my life
It makes the peas taste funny
But it keeps them on the knife.

—Anonymous